The
Perfect
Solution to
Absolutely
Everything

The Perfect Solution to Absolutely Everything

By *Arthur Hoppe*

Edited by William German

DOUBLEDAY & COMPANY, INC., GARDEN CITY, NEW YORK

1968

December, 1968
Design by Jeanette Portelli

Library of Congress Catalog Card Number 68–29644
Copyright © 1968 by Arthur Hoppe
All Rights Reserved
Printed in the United States of America
First Edition

To Leslie, Andrea, Nick and Prentiss . . .
for keeping quiet.

Contents

Part Three
WE, THE WORLD

Part Four
IT, THE WAR

In Gratitude

This book is a collection of columns culled from some 1500 I have written over the past five years. I would like to express my appreciation to Mr. William German, news editor of the San Francisco *Chronicle*, for culling them.

My gratitude to Mr. German is stimulated not only by the excellent job he did, but by the knowledge that some readers will write in to say, "Why did you include that stupid column?" or, more rarely, "Why did you leave such and such a masterpiece out?"

I am, therefore, deeply grateful to have Mr. German to refer them to.

ARTHUR HOPPE

San Francisco
June 5, 1968

Introduction

This is an amazingly simple book. It begins with an amazingly simple solution to every single problem we face today. Then it goes on for a couple of hundred pages to detail the problems this amazing simple solution will solve —such problems as smog, the President, water pollution, General Hershey, racial strife, soil erosion and people who cough during the third act of *Lohengrin*.

The solution is, of course, birth control. *Total* birth control. This will not only solve our problems, but it will solve them in a single generation.

It is up to each of us, then, to do our part to make this a better world by practicing birth control. Indeed, as you look at life each day and at the seemingly insoluble problems you face, what better advice could you seek than to get out there and practice, practice, practice.

ARTHUR HOPPE
Executive Secretary
The League for Total Birth Control

Part One

THEE, THE PEOPLE

The League for Total Birth Control

Practice, Practice, Practice

One grave problem these days is that there are so many controversial subjects you can't talk about without arousing ire, such as politics, religion and sex. So let's talk about a subject on which there is widespread agreement. Let's talk about Motherhood. Just about everyone's against that. For Motherhood, of course, has been directly linked to the dread population explosion, and all thinking people feel the Government should do something about this—such as passing out birth-control pamphlets and the like in a sort of adult vocational program.

But is this moral? Is this Constitutional? Or is it not? This has become one of the great ethical and legal debates of our time. Frankly, I'm not sure I know any of the answers. I'm just part of the problem. But I do feel compelled to say a few words on the burning issue of birth control itself:

It doesn't work.

I fear this one aspect of the burning issue has been somewhat overlooked. It is high time we discussed it openly and frankly, and if the kiddies have left for school, I'd be glad to. First, we must recognize that this Government adult vocational program is basically for poor people—poor, uneducated people. After all, rich, educated people have been practicing it for years, in some rare instances with success.

Thus it's really selective nonbreeding. But that's good. Certainly there is no easier, more efficient way to wipe out poverty and ignorance in future generations than by wiping out the poor and ignorant.

Unfortunately, however, technical details of this vocational program are most difficult to master. Some of my rich, educated friends have flunked the course several times and they've been practicing, practicing, practicing for years. Moreover, we must deal with human (Are you sure the kiddies have left?) passions. Take the Government birth-control lady. There she is, carefully explaining all about pills, thermometers, calendars and various *art nouveau* devices to Mrs. Soandso, who lives in a cold-water flat with her eleven children and an unemployed husband who loves her madly—he not having anything else to do.

Let's face facts. Mrs. Soandso is fervently dedicated to the high concepts of birth control. So is Mr. Soandso. Couldn't be more so. Yet the world is inescapably going to have a lot more little Soandsos. For love, dear friends, conquers all, including the U. S. Constitution, a higher moral law, and Enovid. True, someday a technological breakthrough may provide us with the Perfect Pill, safe, sure and pleasant-tasting. Obviously, it won't be one that works for merely twenty-four hours, not with the way ladies are always losing their purses. But if it's one that's good for, say, forty years, we may lick Motherhood yet.

But, to tell the truth, the whole concept makes me uneasy. It's not so much that I think the whole human race is here by Grand Design. It's that I think at least half the human race is here by accident.

So let us ask ourselves, if this Perfect Pill had been handy a hundred years ago, where would we be today? The odds are ominous. And while I don't know about you, I'd sure miss me.

A Proven System

Hats off to the Upper Classes. They generally have separate bedrooms built into their houses. I think this will solve the population explosion. I'm not, heaven forbid, prying into anyone's personal affairs. I only wish to salute them for helping popularize the only proven-safe, easily understood, guaranteed-effective method of Planned Parenthood. It's what we experts in the field refer to as Geographical Birth Control.

Actually, up to now, it's been a matter of economics. The richer you get, the farther away from your wife you get. The poor, as you know, sleep in double beds. The middle class, in twins. While the rich enjoy separate bedrooms, separate cabanas and separate vacations. This explains why we have so many poor people in the world. And so few rich. So hats off again to our social leaders, I say. For pointing the way through Geographical Birth Control.

For the population explosion, let's face facts, boils down to a question of opportunity. Statistics bear this out irrefutably. The poor, who sleep in double beds, average a shocking 7.2 children per household. Now a few sociologists hold this is due to the lack of outdoorsy leisure-time activities. Such as water polo and quoits. But the double bed's essential responsibility cannot be ignored.

Take the middle class in its twin beds. A far more admirable average of only 2.4 children per household. More quoit players, you say? Perhaps. But the prime factor is that opportunity has been withdrawn a good yard. Or, as Rotarian speakers invariably put it, "Seizing opportunity requires get-up-and-go." But to date the problem has been solved satisfactorily only by the rich. I doubt any more effective method will ever be devised than having to get up on a cold night, fumble in the closet for one's bathrobe and slippers, stumble down a drafty hall and knock three times on a closed door. Only to find she's off someplace on a separate vacation. The very thought quells the spirit of romance. Thus it is no surprise that the Idle Rich, as we call them, average a distinguished 1.2 children. A goal for us all to shoot at.

If the Government wishes to enter the field of birth control, logic dictates that it should promote the only perfect method. And let our battle cry then be: "Separate Bedrooms for the Poor!" With perhaps a few quoits thrown in.

Meanwhile, it is up to us as individuals. Join the Geographical Birth Control League today. Do your part to save the world by stamping out Togetherness.

Eyeball to Eyeball

I'm sorry. I mentioned that whole business about separate bedrooms merely to point out that the richer you get, the farther away from your wife you get. And the fewer children you have. I noted that this was Geographical Birth Control— "the only system," I said flatly, "that really worked." So I opened the next day's Society pages and there were nine blessed events taking place among nine of our most social families, of which only two could be called climbers. Well, it's all my fault. I suppose I should've given more detailed instructions. But that's the whole trouble with all our present complex methods. They require precise directions which you've got to follow to the letter. And in the proper sequence. Or else. Which is why love often conquers all.

But our scientists, thank goodness, are working on it. And I'm deliriously happy to learn that Dr. Carl G. Heller, who's what is called "a reproductive physiologist" at the Pacific Northwest Research Foundation, has made a smashing technological breakthrough. He's come up with a pill for gentlemen that's cheap, safe, harmless to your maleness and guaranteed absolutely 100 percent effective. It even tastes good. In fact, says Dr. Heller, tests show it's got only one teensy little drawback:

If you take a single drink while on the pills, your eyeballs turn bright red.

Thus his new pills, the good doctor told the American Chemical Society sadly, "probably would not be acceptable to men in the Western World." And back he went to the old drawing board.

Nonsense! Here we are, faced with a population explosion and our fainthearted scientists are willing to scrap our salvation. All because of one tiny little flaw. Shades of Thomas Alva Edison! Is this what made America great? No! I say we've got to get out there and sell. For example, we could sell men on the idea of giving up drinking because . . . Well, we could at least sell them on wearing dark glasses to cocktail parties. But, better yet, let's Think Positively. We will simply sell them on red eyeballs.

Actually, when you stop to think about it, there's nothing inherently wrong with red eyeballs. Not that a little good promotion work wouldn't cure. Ads: "ARE YOUR EYEBALLS PALE, TIRED, COLORLESS?" Drinks: "THE RED-EYE HIGHBALL." Contests: "MR. RED-BLOODED AMERICAN EYEBALL."

Of course, the ladies would take a bit of convincing. You know how they are. We might start by planting a few pointed articles in the ladies' magazines. Such as *True Confessions*: "There We Were, Eyeball to Eyeball—And His Were White!" Eventually, I'm sure, we'd convince them of the undeniable advantages of such a method. I mean there you are, an attractive young lady. You walk into a cocktail party crowded with handsome young bachelors. Half have red eyeballs, half don't. Which . . . Well, I don't want to go into details. But we'd soon separate the ladies from the girls. And most bachelors will, I know, agree that's an undeniable advantage there.

Oh, I can hear you saying you don't care. You still don't like red eyeballs. Well let me tell you this is not the time for petty esthetic prejudices. All present methods require diligence. Join your local Red Eyeball League today. And remember our slogan:

"Better Red than Bred!"

Stamp Out People

I do my best to snuff out the population explosion with the Red Eyeball Method of birth control, and now the good ladies of the Planned Parenthood League are mad at me. They say I don't really believe in birth control at all. And that's not true. I'm wholeheartedly for it. In practice.

It's the theory that bothers me. These dire warnings that overpopulation is a graver danger than The Bomb. You know, this constant harping on the theme that the population explosion is going to wipe out the human race. Now I can see the logic of that as well as the next man. Who wants to be wiped out in a population explosion? And I can see where we've got to stop lots of people from being born. For their own good. But by merely limiting births are we shooting high enough? Will birth control, as now envisaged, solve all our problems? Absolutely not. What we need to solve all our problems is Total Birth Control.

Take poverty. Total Birth Control will not merely reduce poverty, it will do away with poverty forever. Not to mention traffic congestion, unglued stamps, busy signals and unsightly roadside litter. And best of all, Total Birth Control will accomplish all this in a single generation!

It just shows you the Power of Negative Thinking. Indeed, no matter how hard I put my mind to it, I can't come up with one solitary problem that Total Birth Control won't eradicate. Urban sprawl? Water pollution? Racial strife? Smog? Lung cancer? Insecticides? Senator Eastland? These seemingly insuperable challenges to humanity will vanish as if by magic. Our rivers will run pure, the wild-flowers will bloom in profusion, the robins will return and the world will be an even more wonderful place in which to live. As soon as we get rid of us people. After all, it's people who cause all the problems we've got now. And if there's one thing we advocates of birth control are right about, it's that the more people we get, the more problems we're going to have. And, of course, the less people we have around, the fewer problems we'll face. You just can't argue with that.

But, even so, our fainthearted planners are all agreed on merely limiting the world population. Like to three billion people. Or maybe three hundred and seventy-four people. Or something. I call this wishy-washy thinking. As long as we have people we're going to have problems. Birth control is certainly no place for halfway measures. As anyone with experience in this field will testify.

But don't misunderstand. I think the Planned Parenthood League is doing a fine job. Within limits. And if you or I wish merely to limit the size of our families, that's our business. As long as we do it strictly for our own sakes. But if you believe birth control is an ideal way to solve the world's problems, then go all out. Join the Total Birth Control League today. Remember our motto:

"Think of the Generations Yet Unborn—Let's Keep Them That Way!"

Love Will Find a Way

As usual, we militant do-gooders in the League for Total Birth Control are far ahead of our wishy-washy rivals in this field. For while they advocate limited controls to reduce some of the world's problems, we demand total control. Which we guarantee will solve all of the world's problems. In a single generation. Nor do we put our faith, as do they, in pills you forget to take, devices you neglect to pack, or calendars you can't see in the dark. No, sir. Our problems cannot be solved, we say, until every nation signs a covenant, similar to the Geneva Convention, renouncing forever the very activities which contribute to the dread population explosion.

What's more, the treaty must include adequate on-site inspection.

It is this last proviso that puts us far ahead of our rivals. For what good, we ask, is even limited population control without adequate on-site inspection? What prevents a nation from cheating? If it does, it will not only come to rule the world, but, worse, it will repopulate it. And then we'll face the same old awful problems we face today. Like having to stand up on the bus.

Nor can we count on the decency of our individual fellow men. Why, the most decent of fellow men may worry all day about the population explosion. But then he espies a fellow lady and—Zingo! There goes the old world. For, oddly enough, statistics show that while we all worry about the population explosion, we don't worry about it at the right time. Thus, the need for on-site inspection in any system of population control is abundantly clear. Oh what a glorious cause. Indeed, I, for one, am prepared to renounce all in order to serve, if need be, as an on-site inspector. Send me, I say bravely, to save the world. Send me, I beg, where the action's hottest. Send me, for example, to Paris.

Ah, there I am, on front-line night patrol in the Bois de Boulogne, creeping through the shrubbery, a wickedly honed pencil between my teeth. Hah! I spy two shadowy figures on the grass. It is clear they are not trying to save the world. I leap forth like a tiger and flash my badge. "Hands up!" I cry. "For I am an on-site inspector."

"*Zut!*" says he. "*Alors!*" says she. "You are cheating," says I. "Not so, we are engaged," says he.

But I whip out my brochure providing that by the year 2172 our population will reach 168,772,834,921,666. If no one is run over by a truck. They naturally repent and, heads held high, march off to save the world. Separately, of course.

I can't tell you the enthusiastic reactions the League's plan for on-site inspections has stimulated. Like: "Well, it's the only activity the Government hasn't controlled yet." Or: "I'd as lief they dropped The Bomb and got it over with." Which, come to think of it, is certainly true. I mean dropping The Bomb would certainly solve precisely the same problems population control will solve. And a lot quicker, too. I'll have to bring it up at the next League meeting. During the Creative Solutions Period.

Let's See Your License

The League for Total Birth Control wishes to announce the presentation of its annual Giant Stride Forward Award to Dr. H. Stanley Glass of Johns Hopkins University. For his plan to license procreation by Government permit. "The right to have children cannot remain unlimited," said the distinguished biologist. (For if it does, of course, we will all be killed in the population explosion.) After applying his scientific mind to this scientific problem, Dr. Glass came up with a perfectly reasonable scientific solution: No one can have a baby without a Government permit. Anyone who does would promptly be sterilized.

Now, as any advocate of solving the world's problems through birth control can see, this is certainly the next logical step. And all that remains is to fill in the details.

(*Scene: The Bureau of Procreation Permits, Department of Agriculture. An eager couple, whom we shall call "Mums" and "Daddy," are standing nervously in line before window 17-C.*)

Mums: Isn't it exciting? Ever since you first told me we were going to have a baby, I've hardly slept. Oh, I loved the way you broke the news, sitting there in your chair, not saying a thing, just filling in application forms and looking smug.

Daddy (squeezing her arm): I'm so glad it made you happy. And now, just think. After nine months of waiting, the big day has finally come. We are going to have our interview.

The Clerk: Next. Okay, have you filled in forms 3703, B-16a and Declaration of Estimated Income?

Daddy: Yes sir, here they are. In quadruplicate.

The Clerk: Okay, you got your high-school transcript, service record, baptismal certificate and blood sample? Good. Now, close your left eye, read the top line on the chart, put your thumb print here, recite the loyalty oath and hold still while the camera takes your picture. Fine. Now what do you want a permit to produce?

Mums: A beautiful golden-haired, rosy-cheeked little girl.

Daddy (at the same time): A fine, strapping, little boy.

Mums (laughing shyly): Oh, either one, really.

The Clerk: A baby? Too bad. We're 7.2 percent over our baby allotment at this time due to accidents and disasters and bootleg production. Will you growers never learn? But fortunately, I can give you an in-lieu license entitling you to produce sixteen pounds of potatoes, three bushels of rutabagas and a hog. Sign here. Next.

It's obvious procreation permits are the coming thing. Telling people what they can produce is very scientific and governmental. But even such a scientific advance is really only a halfway measure to solving the world's problems.

No, only through Total Birth Control can we wipe out all the world's problems. Including scientists who look on human life as a scientific problem.

Ban the Mom

The League for Total Birth Control will hold its annual Mother's Day protest march, effigy burning, and Ban-the-Mom Rally today. In keeping with the spirit of the occasion, all members will wear black arm bands.

"Other well-meaning organizations are advocating limited birth control to solve many of the world's problems," said the League's executive director, Dr. Homer T. Pettibone. "But this is no time for halfway measures. Only Total Birth Control will solve all the world's problems."

Dr. Pettibone said, however, that the League would welcome the support of these other organizations in making Mother's Day a national day of mourning.

"Now that the problem has been so widely recognized," he said, "we feel we can, by all working together, wipe

out once and for all that age-old curse of mankind—
Motherhood."

Not only is Motherhood the sole and direct cause of the
population explosion, said Dr. Pettibone grimly, but every
single problem we face in our daily lives can invariably
be traced to somebody's mother.

"The man who coughs on you in the bus, the fellow who
steals your parking place, the lady who is late for an appointment—exhaustive studies prove beyond doubt that they
all share one thing in common: They all had mothers. Not
only is this true today, but extensive historical research
shows that every evildoer, from Attila the Hun to Adolf
Hitler, had, somewhere in his background, a mother. These
statistics rule out coincidence. There can be no doubt of a
direct link. If we wipe out Motherhood, we will unquestionably wipe out not only overpopulation, but war, soil
erosion, dental caries, air pollution and people who cough
on buses."

Dr. Pettibone paused to wipe off his pince-nez, which
had steamed up. "Thus, it is our duty to convince an un-
caring public of the simple fact," he said, "that the hand
that rocks the cradle rocks the boat.

"In our ceremonies today we will honor Miss Hettie
Hornsmuth, a barren spinster of seventy-eight, as Mother
of the Year in tribute to her lifelong restraint in not adding
to the problems of mankind. As usual, we will collect
funds for our Permanent Home for Unwed Non-mothers.
We will pass out literature urging all young ladies: 'Don't
Be a Mother, Be a Sport.' And, in that regard, we will

honor the developers of The Pill under our new slogan: 'A Better World Through Chemistry.'"

At this point, Dr. Pettibone was asked if there had not been one mother somewhere since the dawn of time who had benefited the world—one mother whose act of creation he wholeheartedly approved.

"Oh, yes," said Dr. Pettibone simply. "Mine."

Let's Be Extinct

Like all militant do-gooders, we dedicated members of The League for Total Birth Control have our detractors. You know what they're calling us? "A bunch of fuzzy-minded idealists," that's what.

"It's true," writes a snide critic, "that Total Birth Control would wipe out hunger, poverty and war in a single generation. But our present pills, devices and other methods simply can't achieve such perfection. You daydreamers are technologically way ahead of your time."

Perhaps this was true only yesterday. But today, thanks to the American Cynamid Company of Wayne, New Jersey, saving the world is within our grasp. For American Cynamid has just announced it's on the verge of a smashing break-through—a new chemical which will "render an unwanted species extinct in a relatively short period of time." And what, I ask you, is the most unwanted species around these days? Oh, I can hardly wait.

Naturally, these new chemicals which offer so much hope

aren't poisons. All we advocates of population control agree that going around poisoning surplus human beings would be highly immoral. No sir, they're called "chemosterilants." And all they do is sterilize an unwanted species. Which, of course, is the most effective birth-control method of all. Once such a boon is perfected, all we'll have to do is spray the world with it. Presto! Instant birth control.

How neat, how simple, how clean. No wrangling over on-site inspections to prevent cheating. No trying to teach the Hottentot's wife the mysteries of the calendar. No solemn arguments over religious scruples. And just envision how much better the world will grow, year by year. At first you'll hardly notice. But in nine months we'll be able to convert our maternity wards to ease the growing shortage of hospital beds. In five years we'll begin to lick the desperate overcrowding of our schools. In sixteen, the number of drivers will start declining, inexorably reducing pedestrian fatalities, traffic jams and general nervous tension. As the years pass, life will grow better and better. There'll be empty seats on every bus, empty tables in every restaurant, empty parking places on every street and plenty of closet space for all. As our sprawling suburbs shrink, so will the time wasted on commuting. As the cubic space available to each of us grows, so will we have more room to dance and play and leap for joy.

Ever fewer picnickers will despoil our wilderness. Ever fewer farmers will erode our soil. Ever fewer factory chimneys will cloud our air. Ever fewer people will pollute our streams. What a beautiful world it will be to live in, problem-free, crystal-clean. It's a shame nobody will be around to enjoy it. Indeed, you can't help feeling a bit sorry for those generations yet unborn. Who won't be.

But think of how far, far better life will be for all of us lucky enough to be enjoying it now. And after all, that's the whole point of birth control. Isn't it?

Don't Trust Anyone Under Thirty

Please Practice What We Preach

"From these failing hands we pass the torch . . ." No, that's been said. "As you go forth into the world . . ." What? Excuse my nervousness, but I've been invited to deliver the commencement address at my alma mater. It's a high honor and a grave responsibility. True, this particular alma mater is a very small grammar school I happened to attend. And the graduating class consists of ten young men and women not yet full-grown. But it's part of the national scene. Across the land, our tired old generation is standing on rostrums describing to the eager new generation what the world we have worked so hard to create for them is like. And how best to cope with this terrible situation.

Fortunately, like most members of my tired old generation, I am loaded up to here with good advice. I give it to myself all the time. And I will be glad to share the good advice I give myself with the eager new generation. Excerpts follow.

As I look over this vast sea of ten young faces today, allow me to impart a few words of wisdom which may be of help to you as you embark upon your voyage through life: Follow not the primrose path, to thine own self be true, and don't forget to brush your teeth after every meal.

Above all, speak out for what you believe in. Quit smoking. Love all living things. Don't eat so much fatty food. Always question the conventional wisdom. Remember to do your Royal Canadian Air Force exercises every morning. Live life to its very fullest without hurting anybody. And fix leaky faucets just as soon as they start to drip. Never waste your time reading trashy books or watching trashy television shows, for you have only so much time to live. Get more sleep. Treasure every individual in the world, but be suspicious of all groups from garden clubs to nations. Clean your paint brushes right after using.

Always wear your safety belt when driving. Try to love for its own sake and not because you expect love in return. Stop putting off getting your annual checkup. When anyone says the world is an awful place, always ask, "Compared to what?" Balance your checkbook every single month, one way or another. Avoid cluttering up your life with material possessions. Relax in traffic. Play the exciting games of politics or business for the chips of power or money, but remember they are basically only games and not nearly so real or so valuable as the laughter of children, warm sunshine or eating when you are hungry. And don't drink after dinner, because it gives you a hangover.

Fight for peace, don't take pills, hate hatred, cut down on coffee, stop . . .

Stop! It's not good. I am regretfully declining this invitation to give a lot of good advice to the eager new generation. I think it's all great advice. But I can see now that they won't follow it. Either. And if they won't follow our advice there isn't much hope for them. No sir, they're going to grow up just like us.

We Shall Be Overcome

Here's the Right Wing warning us of sneaky Communist plots. And there's the Left Wing decrying the insidious John Birch conspiracy. But I, personally, have discovered a subversive threat which makes all others pale into insignificance. This conspiracy is so vast it staggers the imagination. Its devoted members are dedicated enemies of virtually all we hold near and dear. And their collective goal, make no mistake, is the eventual takeover of our society so that they may still survive.

Already, fellow Americans, they are everywhere among us. To spread their poisonous propaganda they have infiltrated Hollywood, pre-empted prime television time, and all but taken over our great American record industry. Worst of all, their conscious agents have wormed their way into the bosoms of millions of American households, where they seek, night and day, to brainwash us to their strange ways. I am speaking, of course, fellow grownups, of our American youths.

Frankly, the first inkling I had of this plot by our young people was when I saw a picture of one at the University of California demonstrations carrying a placard which read: "DON'T TRUST ANYONE OVER THIRTY!" How typical, I remember thinking, of this younger generation. Then later, I heard their leading folk singer, Mr. Bob Dylan. Do you know what he sings about? He sings about how badly we've loused things up and how we'd better get out of the way because they're going to take over. A *Mein Kampf*, if I've ever heard one.

Ever since, I've been putting bits and pieces together, and at last I feel ready to reveal the entire, shocking picture of this omnipresent conspiracy. Members are apparently admitted about the age of thirteen. At first, they are trained in small acts of rebellion. They learn to reject the way we dress, the way we dance and even the way we talk. Together, they conspire daily to overthrow our cherished standards of neatness and grooming and even our most elementary dietary habits. By the time they are seventeen or eighteen, those who have proven themselves in this basic training are deemed ready to enter politics. Some join the Radical Left, some the Radical Right. And only the most apathetic misfits in their midst align themselves with our hallowed American middle-of-the-road position.

Right or Left, it matters little. For these hard-core militants are united by a common concept shared by every fiery revolutionary since time immemorial. Yes, fellow grown-ups: They burn with the subversive theory that they can run things better than we can. But most appalling of all is the one factor that distinguishes this vast conspiracy from all the other vast ones threatening us: This vast conspiracy is going to win!

Fellow grownups, there can be no doubt that these militant young revolutionaries now among us are going to take over the country. In forty years at the outside. May heaven have mercy on us all.

Our Flaming Elders

The regular monthly meeting of The Never Trust Anybody Over Thirty Club was held yesterday at the Campus Ice Cream a Go-go Parlor. The topic under discussion was: "Are Middle-aged Sociologists Sexually Mature?"

"Absolutely not!" Miss Betty Koed, an attractive blonde, said indignantly. "Why, I can't even go out of the dorm without one of them sneaking up on me with pencil and pad wanting to know if I believe in making out. How often? How far? With whom? Really, their attitude simply reeks of voyeurism. At best."

"In all fairness," said Tim Swift, who is considered something of an apologist for his elders, "they're merely products of their generation. Look how older people are currently preoccupied with four-letter words. They hardly talk about anything else. Now, we may think this is unhealthy . . ."

"I think it's disgusting!" said Betty.

". . . but shouldn't we stop condemning them and try harder to understand them?"

"I think" said Jock Armstrong, the thinker of the group, "the problem's basically simple: They have too much freedom and not enough responsibility."

"Jock's absolutely right!" cried Betty. "Just look at the papers. The number of adults involved in robberies, murders, divorces and drunk-driving arrests is shocking. They have the freedom to carry guns, choose their spouses and drink, but they don't have the responsibility to behave maturely."

"Now, just a minute," said Tim. "That's not fair. You know the papers play up the wild things adults do. But they rarely mention the many, many, good, decent, well-behaved adults. This is what gives society a false picture of what adults are really like today."

"Oh, Tim," said Betty, "just look at the way they're slaves to the latest fad. The men wear ties and jackets on the hottest days. The women are worse. Think of the odd things they eat on their strange diets. And their music! Have you ever listened to them playing their Guy Lombardo records? It'll drive you smack out of your mind. No, precious few adults are responsible enough individuals to dare break the bonds of group conformity."

"I think," said Jock, thoughtfully, "their political behavior is even more appalling. For example, most support the war in Vietnam, which is their right. But how many of them get out there and demonstrate their support through marching, picketings or lie-ins? None. For that matter, how many even bother to vote. Talk about apathy and irresponsibility! As would-be citizens, they're a national disgrace."

The meeting broke up after the members voted overwhelmingly to seek a foundation grant for a study of the sexual habits of middle-aged sociologists—"a step," as Betty put it, "toward understanding the older generation." But the mood was pessimistic. As Jock said, "Even if we ever do understand what makes them wild, pleasure-seeking, irresponsible faddists, what can we do about it?"

"Well," Tim said weakly, "I guess we just have to have faith that, with time, they'll somehow grow more mature."

Four Fables

I.

Sam and the Rutabagas

Once upon a time there was a little boy named Sam. He was a good little boy and did almost everything his father told him to do. When his father said, "Brush your teeth," he brushed his teeth. When his father said, "Eat your rutabaga," he ate his rutabaga. And so forth. Each time he did what his father said, his father was very, very happy. As for Sam, he liked making his father happy. But he never did learn to care much for rutabaga.

Of course, like most little boys, Sam sometimes didn't do what he was told. Once he chewed gum in school. Once he went swimming in the abandoned quarry. And once he rode his bicycle in the street. All of which he enjoyed much more than eating rutabaga. Each time Sam's father heard of such transgressions, he would look up from his bills and say, "Dammit, you must learn more respect for authority." When Sam asked why, his father would snap, "Because I say so." Or, "Shut up and eat your rutabaga."

Determined to learn why he should respect authority, Sam went to the greatest university in the whole wide world. It had lots and lots of authority. The Regents, the President, the Chancellor and all the Deans were for authority. The faculty wrote long dissertations on "The Role of Authority in a Free Society," a problem they examined minutely from every conceivable angle. But the students, of course, were against authority. They were for freedom.

"Freedom," cried Sam, "is much better than authority!" He joined the Free Speech Movement, the Free Sex League, and cadged free lunches whenever possible. He wrote free verse, practiced free love, and passed out anarchist pamphlets in his free time. He grew a beard because the authorities didn't like beards, and wore sandals because the authorities didn't like sandals. Sometimes he didn't brush his teeth for two days running and he swore never, never to eat another rutabaga as long as he lived.

He was very, very happy.

The authorities, of course, said, "Dammit, you must learn more respect for authority." But Sam didn't care because he was happy and he liked freedom better. And his girl friend, Nellie Jo, agreed. They agreed on everything. In fact, when Sam graduated, they agreed to get married. Sam got a job to support them and bought a house for them to live in and an electric toothbrush to brush their teeth with. In time, Sam Junior came along. But he was a good little boy and did almost everything his father told him to do. Which made his father very, very happy. Of course, sometimes Sam Junior didn't do what he was told. When this happened Sam would look up from his bills and say, "Dammit, you've got to learn more respect for authority."

Moral: This is truly the best of all possible worlds. The young like freedom and the old like authority. Thus each of us is happy with what he's got.

II.

The Day the World Was Saved

Once upon a time there was a student organization dedicated to such academic pursuits as philosophy, socioeconomic debating and mass sit-ins. Its name was The Never Trust Anybody Over Thirty Club. Its battle cry was "Never!" And each member always carried a placard saying, "SHAME!", in the event a demonstration should start on any subject whatsoever. Due to the dedication, zeal and around-the-clock activism of its members, the Club was instrumental in molding public opinion. This public opinion was constantly expressed in letters to the editors of the local press: "Why don't those dirty beatniks wash their hair?" And such.

One day the Club discovered with absolute certainty that,

unless something were done, the world would come to an end a week from next Tuesday. A mass lie-in was held on The White House lawn. The demonstrators, with unprecedented fervor, cried, "Never!" "Shame!" and sang, in four-part harmony, "We Shall Not Be Moved." They were, of course. By the cops.

Naturally, nobody listened to what they had to say. Passers-by scuttled around the scene with disdainful looks. Some shook their heads at the sight of so many bearded young men and black-stockinged young ladies. A few paused to shout, "Why don't you dirty beatniks wash your hair?" And such. Photographers took several pictures of the young ladies being dragged off with their skirts above their knees. And a tired reporter wrote a brief caption about another mass arrest of slovenly dressed demonstrators who were apparently in favor of legalizing marijuana.

While accustomed to such reaction, this time the Club called an emergency meeting. "Friends," said Club President Jock Armstrong, scratching his beard, "we know definitely that, unless something is done, the world will come to an end a week from next Tuesday. Yet no one will listen to us. There is but one thing to do. It is a great sacrifice, but I think saving the world is worth it."

There were cries of "Never!" and "Shame!" out of force of habit. But the motion was carried and the members all went home—the young men to shave and the young ladies to put their hair up in curlers. The next day the demonstrators appeared again in front of the White House. But this time the young men wore button-down collars, Ivy League suits and conservatively striped ties. And the young ladies wore nylon stockings, pointy-toed pumps and basic black with pearls. Instead of carrying placards, they politely handed out expensively printed leaflets while softly humming "The Star Spangled Banner." The leaflets said: "As concerned citizens, we wish to view with alarm the impending danger of the world coming to an end a week from next Tuesday and we respectfully suggest something be done."

Passers-by smiled at these well-dressed young people, accepted their leaflets and often paused to chat. The newspapers picked up the story, the President was informed, something was done and the world was saved. Just in the nick of time, too.

Moral: In this great land the cornerstone of our unalienable individual liberties is that every man is entitled to be heard. As long as he dresses decently.

III.

The Day the Students Won

Once upon a time there was a young man named Mario Aptheker Rebel, who went to a great big university. It was a very fine university, everybody said, because it had a lot of prize-winning teachers who didn't teach anything and a lot of marvelous computers which could handle the problems of the students without fuss, muss or bother. But young Mr. Rebel didn't like it. He wasn't sure exactly

what he didn't like, but he didn't like it. And, surprisingly
enough, many other students felt the same way.

So when he called a demonstration, thousands demon-
strated. And before you knew it, there were arrests, riots,
demands, sit-ins, counterproposals, marches, rallies, strikes
and nonviolent rock-and-roll protest songfests. Chancellors
fell. Governors went down to defeat. The whole social
fabric of the nation seemed threatened. The prize-winning
teachers didn't know what to do. The computers blinked,
shuddered and short-circuited. With the University doomed
and nothing to lose, the Regents decided to take the one-
word advice of a precocious office boy: "Approve."

Thus it was that the University President appeared personally at the very next daily noon-rally-and-sleep-in. Lick-
ing his lips nervously, he said:

"All your demands, whatever they may be, are hereby
granted! (*Cheers*) We have come to recognize at last that
the traditional role of students in a democratic society is
to protest the status quo. (*Hearty applause*) And to aid
you we are forthwith appointing Mr. Mario Aptheker
Rebel to the new position of Vice Chancellor in Charge
of Protests." (*Standing ovation*)

Flushed with victory, Mr. Rebel accepted the high post
with glee. "If I could cause all this fuss operating out of
an off-campus garret," he said, rubbing his hands, "think
what I'll be able to do with three secretaries, four telephones and the prestige of this great university behind me."

So Mr. Rebel marched into his carpeted office, plunked
down in his big leather chair and called in his first secretary to dictate a ringing Student Manifesto for All-Out

Rebellion. But his first secretary said it was time for her coffee break. His second secretary was taking her accrued annual sick leave. And his third secretary said, Gee, somebody has to answer the phones. Which reminded her, the Chancellor was on extension seven, the janitor on six, three photographers were in the reception room, and he was due in three minutes at a meeting of department heads to discuss lowering the retirement age of department heads. Mr. Rebel never did get his manifesto written. Which, as he came to see, was just as well, because it might have affected his tenure.

Not that the students cared. After all, it wasn't much fun protesting against authorities who approved of your protesting. The students went back to their classes. The prize-winning teachers went back to not teaching. And the great University's computers whirred smoothly on, handling all problems with no fuss, muss or bother.

Moral: A dedicated rebel can survive any disaster—any disaster but victory.

IV.

Happiness Is Not a Movement

Once upon a time there was a group called The Happiness Movement. At first, it was a very small group. Its members were called Happies. And they were different from everybody else.

"We have discovered something called Love," they announced proudly. "We have invented something called Individual Freedom. We care not what an intolerant, bigoted hypocritical society may think. All we ask is to be left alone."

So all the Happies wore striped bathing suits to signify Individual Freedom, dandelions in their hair to symbolize Love, and bones in their noses because they felt they should return to the simple ways of Cro-Magnon man. Pills to make them happy. Which they were. Not only were the Happies happy, but much of what they said rang true: Love is good, intolerance is bad, freedom's fine, and there's no sweeter right than the right to be left alone. Naturally, society was offended.

"Why can't they take more baths?" growled the Conservatives. "Don't they know cleanliness is next to patriotism?"

"They're right, of course, that we are guilty of everything there is to be guilty about," said the Liberals guiltily. "But why do they have to eat all those pills?"

Naturally, this opprobium stirred every magazine and newspaper to send a disguised reporter to record the Happy philosophy. In addition, the ranks of the movement were swelled by countless teen-agers who thought sex was Love, a striped bathing suit was Freedom, and a Happiness Pill was just the greatest. As they watched their movement grow by leaps and bounds, the Happies were at first pleased, then awed, and at last convinced that they were The Wave of the Future. Where at first they had diffidently offered their doctrines as personal opinion, they now preached them vociferously as divine revelation.

"Anybody who wears a tie instead of a striped bathing

suit is an up-tight, know-nothing enemy of Individual Freedom!" they said bigotedly.

"Anybody who hasn't taken a Happiness Pill can't talk about happiness!" they said intolerantly.

"Anybody who doesn't practice Love the way we practice Love is to be despised!" they said hypocritically.

So it was that the Happies naturally developed the attributes of any successful movement: Its members felt superior to nonmembers; they were convinced of the righteousness of their own dogma; and they were united by a common hatred. Naturally, they no longer talked of changing themselves, but of changing everybody else instead. Naturally, they no longer demanded to be left alone, but marched off to remold society instead.

And naturally, this made them pretty much the same as everybody else.

Moral: The only good movement is one that isn't going anywhere.

Tune In, Turn On, Pass Out

The Drinking School

As a concerned parent and outraged citizen, I am concerned and outraged over the drinking problem among our college youth. Why can't they be more like us? Instead, there they are, out marching, demonstrating and otherwise stirring up trouble over the sober political issues of the day. Their problem, obviously, is they don't drink enough. I'm glad, therefore, to report this little-recognized problem is at last getting the recognition it deserves. A research sociologist, Mr. Ira H. Cisin, says our colleges should teach students how to drink.

"Drinking," he says, "can be dangerous, and the young deserve to be instructed in its uses just as they are taught to swim and drive a car."

Exactly. And as a lifelong expert in the field, I'm naturally applying for a full professorship. Indeed, I've already drawn up my lecture notes for my first class in Drinking 123a (no prerequisites required).

"Good morning, students. Welcome to Drinking 123a. Let me begin by warning you this is no snap course. You may have easily mastered integral calculus, Etruscan epic poetry and advanced thermodynamics, but you now must face the greatest challenge of your academic career: learning how to drink.

"The first seemingly overwhelming obstacle you must surmount in learning to drink alcoholic beverages is that they don't taste good. Not to the beginner. And my advice to you on this point is to choose the beverage you dislike least. For example, some beginners find they dislike Scotch less than they dislike bourbon, gin or rye. Thus, by mixing twenty-year-old Scotch with ginger ale, soda pop or cherry cough syrup, they find they can get it down with only the very mildest of shudders. Just remember that with liquor, the taste is the thing. And you can avoid it if you really try.

"Now, then, let us turn to the effect alcohol will have on you. It is not true that alcohol merely makes you dizzy. It also makes you stupid. Some improperly motivated students, feeling stupid and dizzy, will quit right there. Don't be a dropout! Persevere and you will be rewarded by becoming completely irresponsible. Not to mention violently ill. Of course, becoming violently ill doesn't sound too pleasant. But actually, you'll find you're so dizzy, stupid and irresponsible at this point that it won't matter a whit. It's the next morning that matters. There's no point describing in advance the sensations you'll feel the next morning. For one thing, they're indescribable. Just keep in mind the legend of Robert Bruce and the spider. And each time you fall flat on your face, pick yourself up and try again.

"The course will also cover such related subjects as dry sweats, cold sweats, headaches, tremors, personal injury suits, the Penal Code and various symptoms of the manic depressive. The final exam will be a simulated cocktail party at which you will be asked to down seven lukewarm martinis while listening to a two-hour speech in Urdu. Now, then, as to delirium tremens . . ."

No, I can't face it. It's a hopeless task, I say, to lead our militant young people to drink—much as it would contribute to peace on our campuses. Let's be tolerant and let them go on getting even more involved in politics. That way, they'll be driven to it.

Legalize the Banana

Following is another unwritten chapter in that unpublished reference book *A History of the World, 1950-1999*. The title of this one is "The Great Banana Split."

The news from Berkeley, California, in March of 1967, that hippies had discovered psychedelic properties in the common banana caused grave concern. The gravest concern, of course, was that the banana was perfectly legal. Hippies would scrape the inside of the banana skin, dry the scrapings and smoke them—a painstaking process known as "taking a trip on a banana peel." But with further research a simple recipe was developed for a banana split, best summed up by the slogan: "First you take a banana, then you split."

Banana-split parlors opened coast-to-coast; "Banana Surprise" was served at all jet-set parties; and Chiquita Banana was revived, now wearing ironed hair and leotards, to sing hourly over the radio, "Don't Put Bananas in the Refrigerator (Put them in the humidor, instead)."

"Do you realize," thundered moralists, "that bananas are being openly sold in our once sacrosanct grocery stores?"

But police were powerless. It had taken an Act of Congress to outlaw LSD, and it would take another to ban the banana. A bill was introduced and emergency hearings were begun before the Congressional Committee on Morality, whose chairman interrupted his annual round-the-world trip to investigate sin, vice and dancing girls firsthand, in order to be present for news photographers. The State Department testified that a banana ban would "seriously impair our friendly relations with our great sister republics to the South" and the United Fruit Company.

The President, however, was firm. "I will go anywhere at any time to talk to anyone about morality," he said, "unless there are reasons I don't think I should."

This prompted the junior Senator from New York to make a bold speech saying he was for morality and also for bananas and also for young people, who were reaching voting age in ever increasing numbers. At last, after only eight months' debate, Congress voted. As always, it voted overwhelmingly in favor of morality. All the Congressmen then went off on junkets and the Great Banana Ban went into effect. Hundreds were arrested for selling, possessing or smoking bananas. Moralists relaxed. "The country is saved," they said. That's when a hippie in Omaha City discovered that Swiss chard and marshmallow sauce turned you on.

The Swiss Chard Ban the following year was hailed by moralists and small children. In succeeding years, Congress, desperately trying to keep up with research, outlawed potatoes, tomatoes and all health foods, one by one. But when a mixture of mother's milk and yogurt was found psychedelic, Congressmen threw up their hands.

"You can't attack mother's milk," said one.

Finally, in reaction, a bill was passed saying anybody could eat, drink or smoke anything he liked as long as he didn't hurt anybody else. Oddly enough, about the same small percentage of people who wanted to turn on, went on turning on. And the vast majority who didn't, didn't.

The only difference was that turning on wasn't nearly as thrilling.

The New Middle-agers

(Scene: The Gray Submarine, a noted hangout for members of what has come to be known as "The New Middle-agers." In this dim, smoky light, men and women, most of them in their forties, can be seen lounging about in chairs and sofas. A sign on the wall says, "Never Trust Anybody Over Sixty.")

The group's leader, Dr. Timothy Leering, peers into an ordinary-looking brown paper bag somewhat furtively and speaks.)

Dr. Leering: We've got the real, genuine stuff tonight, gang. There's enough here for everybody to turn on.

Bob Babbitt (hopefully): Marijuana? I've always wanted to smoke some marijuana.

Dr. Leering (testily): Smoking marijuana is kid stuff. You've got to face up to the fact that you're too old to be a hippie.

Bob Babbitt (defensively): I just wanted to see what it was like. I mean it's not habit-forming. And it doesn't cause emphysema, heart disease or lung cancer.

Dr. Leering: Exactly. It has no permanent effect on you whatsoever. You merely achieve a temporary state of euphoria which goes away, leaving you the same middle-aged slob you were before.

Bob Babbitt (hanging his head): I guess I wasn't thinking.

Dr. Leering (offering a filter-tip cigarette): If you want to smoke, smoke these. Remember our motto: "I'd Rather Die Than Switch."

Daphne Darling (excitedly): But tell us about the stuff in the bag, Doctor. Will we really turn on?

Dr. Leering: At the very least, I think I can guarantee you a genuine psychosomatic experience. *(frowning)* Of course, I should warn you that you may have a bad trip.

Bob Babbitt (nervously): A bad trip? What's that?

Dr. Leering: Well, it affects people differently. There's a chance it may just make you nauseated. Or it may strike the central nervous system, causing tremors, syncope, paralysis and even death.

Daphne Darling (*with a delicious shudder*): Oooo! And will we became addicts?

Dr. Leering: Some of you will. In that case, you will develop a physiological tolerance, experience acute withdrawal symptoms and hallucinations and suffer permanent brain damage.

Bob Babbitt (*dubiously*): Golly, I don't know if . . .

Dr. Leering (*with fervor*): Have courage, Babbitt! Remember that it's a symbol to us Middle-agers of our rebellion against the oppressions and frustrations of these crass times in which we live.

Bob Babbitt: I don't see why marijuana . . .

Dr. Leering (*angrily*): Act your age, Babbitt. Marijuana's illegal.

Daphne Darling (*trembling*): Oh, please Doctor. Please give it to us now.

Dr. Leering (mollified): All right. But it's most important that it be prepared with extreme care. (*removing two bottles from the bag*) Now, let's see—eight parts gin, one part vermouth, a twist of lemon . . .

The Real Stuff

In the furor over LSD and other hallucinating drugs, our leaders have ignored the discovery of a new "thrill pill" which threatens to destroy utterly our present way of life.

The new drug, known as LS-MFD, was first isolated and synthesized by the noted researcher Dr. Tom Hicks. Its major ingredient is a leading antacid compound and it can be made by any high-school chemistry student. And what are the insidious effects of LS-MFD on the thrill seeker who ingests as little as 100 milligrams in a sugar cube?

"It causes him," said Dr. Hicks with a suppressed shudder, "to experience reality."

Already, there is a rapidly growing group of users, known as "alka-heads," who show an almost religious devotion to the effects of the drug—an experience they describe in their argot as "staying where you are" or "turning off."

Here, in the words of one alka-head, Homer T. —————, is what such a "stay" can be like:

"I had a tough day at the office. So when I got home I decided to take a stay. Nothing happened for about twenty minutes. And then this indescribable feeling came over me. The first thing I did was to get up and turn off the television set. I poured my martini down the sink and went out into the back yard. I'd never really noticed before how sun-warmed the earth is in the late afternoon and how a leaf is made and the way a cabbage moth flies. It was beautiful.

"My wife asked if I was going bowling and I said no, because it really didn't make sense to knock over pins with a ball for hours on end. I said I'd rather go downtown and look at people. I did and it made me a little sad the way nobody looks in your eyes. But I was very excited to see how many different kinds of people there are—old, young, rich, poor. Every single one of them different! I went home, kissed my wife, played happily with my children and went off to sleep without a sedative."

Unfortunately, as sometimes happens, Mr. —————— suffered brief, recurring periods of reality for several weeks following. One occurred at the office during a conference to think up a new slogan for a stick-type deodorant. He was fired.

Not only can LS-MFD cause unpleasant after-effects, but it can also result in a "bad stay." In one such case the user picked up a newspaper while he was turned off. He was found later wandering down the street in a daze muttering, "We're *really* killing *real* people in Vietnam."

Thus, while society applauds our leaders for cracking down on LSD and other mind-expanding drugs, the spreading use of LS-MFD poses a far greater threat. Not only will it wipe out the great television, alcohol and bowling industries, but its potential for causing psychic damage is far greater.

For most of us are unquestionably conditioned from birth to survive hallucinations. But who's equipped to face reality?

The Perfect Pill

Once upon a time there was a young man named Aristotle Spinoza who wanted to save the human race. So he dropped out.

"Cleanliness is overrated," said Aristotle to himself.

"Social taboos against long hair are silly. It's hate, greed and striving that ruin the world. The human race will never be saved until we all come to love each other."

So he gave up baths, grew his hair long and went to live in a hippie pad. Right away, Aristotle ran into several minor problems and one major one. The minor ones included underarm offensiveness, an itchy neck and chronic indigestion. The major one was that, try as he might, he couldn't bring himself to love everybody—particularly one bearded roommate given to playing the sitar at 2 A.M. and eating crackers in bed.

Aristotle took his problems to a guru. "Hmmm," said the guru, "how many micrograms of acid are you taking?"

"Acid?" asked Aristotle.

"Lysergic acid. LSD. It will increase your awareness, expand your consciousness, and you will love everybody," said the guru solemnly. "Take 250 micrograms twice weekly four hours after eating. Next."

And it worked! After taking LSD, Aristotle saw pretty colors, heard pretty sounds, smelled pretty smells, felt pretty feelings and loved everybody. He even equated the noise of crackers being munched in bed with Beethoven's Fifth Symphony. But these effects wore off in eight hours. And most of the time he itched, smelled, burped and couldn't stand sitar music.

"LSD is fine, but it isn't perfect," he said thoughtfully. "What the human race needs is The Perfect Pill."

After many an experiment, he invented it. The Perfect Pill contained an itch reliever, a deodorant, an antacid tablet and, unlike LSD, it turned you on permanently. The Perfect

Pill was an instant success. Soon everybody in the world was turned on permanently. Hate, greed, striving and silly social taboos disappeared. Everybody sat around seeing pretty colors, listening to pretty sounds, smelling pretty smells, feeling pretty feelings and loving each other.

Of course, while no one bothered to go to war any more, no one bothered to build bridges, have children or explore the universe any more, either. And after a few hundred years of sitting around loving each other the human race died off. It was replaced by the three-toed sloth, a gentle creature. "It's your bag now," said the last man to the three-toed sloth. "But I notice you don't take pills. Have you found some better way to love each other?"

"Naturally," said the three-toed sloth.

Moral: If the only way people can be induced to love one another is through ingesting chemicals the human race deserves what it gets.

Sex Is a Four-letter Word

In the Beginning Was the Word

It was in the third year of the reign of Alaric the Square (223–207 B.C.), King of all the Angles and Saxons, that the historic Obscenity Trials swept the land. Most typical, perhaps, was that of Miss Demmorrah Muldoon, the famed "Love Poetess." She was arrested and jailed after writing a poem which read:

> When the dew is on the buttercup,
> I yearn to xptl with you.

What outraged moralists, of course, was Miss Muldoon's bold use of the ancient four-letter Druid word "xptl," hitherto seen only on men's-room walls.

"Miss Muldoon is guilty of pandering to the decadence

gnawing at our society by deliberately employing the obscene Druid word '——,'" wrote an incensed editorial writer. "After all, there is a perfectly good four-letter Anglo-Saxon word that adequately describes this act."

As sales of Miss Muldoon's poem passed the million mark, her trial opened.

"We will prove," thundered the grim-faced prosecutor, "that this poem violates contemporary community standards of morality, appeals solely to the prurient interest and is utterly without redeeming social importance."

His first witnesses were the two veteran police officers who arrested Miss Muldoon. Both said blushingly that they had never been so shocked and embarrassed in their lives as upon seeing "xptl" on other than a men's-room wall. And one testified he hadn't been able to look any female in the eye since. Next came a high priest who, as an expert witness, said that no husband ever would use the word "xptl" with his wife. He added that he certainly wouldn't—granted that his church allowed him to marry, which, thank heaven, it didn't—even if he knew what it meant. Last was a famed physician known far and wide for his treatment of mental disorders. He said the very word "xptl" would drive his patients crazy. And as for himself, he said, hearing the word filled him with shame, loathing, disgust, feelings of inadequacy, a hatred of his mother with whom he still lived, and an overwhelming desire to eat peanut butter sandwiches.

The defense countered a learned professor of literature who pronounced the poem "an ennobling and spiritually uplifting classic that depended for its eternal verity on the single word 'xptl.'" After a two-week trial, the jury of twelve ox-cart drivers and mule-skinners took thirteen minutes to find Miss Muldoon guilty of "attempting to destroy our cherished Anglo-Saxon heritage." She was beheaded on May 24, 220 B.C.—her last defiant words being: "History will absolve me! Xptl you all!"

But thanks to the example made of Miss Muldoon, no Anglo-Saxon writer ever again dared employ the ancient Druid word "xptl," and it fell to disuse. Instead, much to the gratification of moralists, they stuck to common, ordinary, garden-variety words that could be clearly spelled out anywhere in the land without giving offense.

You know, four-letter Anglo-Saxon words like "——," "——," and "——."

Don't Shout It

Once upon a time there was a little boy named Sam. He was a nice, polite little boy, but he knew a four-letter word. One day, Sam mentioned the word aloud in front of a playmate. The playmate covered his ears, ran home and was never allowed to play with Sam again. "How strange," said Sam. "It is only a word and can do no harm."

So he asked his mother, "Mother dear, why is the word . . ." Before he could finish, his mother boxed his ears, scrubbed out his mouth with soap and turned off television. Hurt by such unfair treatment, Sam cornered his father when he came home. "Father dear," he said, "certainly it can cause no harm to say . . ." His father grabbed him by the collar, whacked him with a hairbrush and locked him in his room. Sam vowed never ever to say the word ever ever again. But at the age of seventeen, Sam fell in love. And one day, as dreamy lovers will, he forgot his vow and casually dropped the word in the presence of his beloved. She slapped his face. "Oh tell me," pleaded Sam desperately, "how can this harmless little word hurt you?" But she never spoke to him again.

Broken-hearted, Sam pledged to devote his life to studying the secret of this little word to discover its evil power. And he enrolled in the biggest, greatest, grandest university in the whole wide world. He studied history to see if the little word had caused any wars. He studied geography to see if it were perhaps the name of some awful country. And finally he studied physiology and acoustics. "For," he said, "it is obvious that the sound waves of this little word must somehow derange the minds of those who hear it." For three years he toiled. He tested the word on white mice, anacondas and rhesus monkeys. He proved conclusively that the word caused no more physical damage than *love, bomb* or *antidisestablishmentarianism.*" At last, he went to his Kindly Old Professor. "I was right all along," he said proudly. "This word is historically, geographically and scientifically absolutely harmless. I could shout it from the window without causing the slightest damage to anyone or anything."

"Oh, please don't," said the Kindly Old Professor with a shudder. But Sam, determined to prove his point, opened the window, took a deep breath and with all his might cried out: "XPTL!"

The President and the Chancellor of the biggest, greatest, grandest university in the whole wide world immediately resigned. The Regents demanded 10,000 students be expelled. The Alumni stopped their checks. Every newspaper decried and deplored. The Legislature launched a thorough investigation. And the prospects of the Governor for re-election were seriously dimmed. Sam surveyed the wreckage sadly, told the Kindly Old Professor he was very, very, sorry and went off to become a Trappist monk.

Moral: Some fables you just wouldn't believe.

Me, Dick; You, Jane

Sex education, I'm glad to say, offers many growing opportunities. San Jose, California, for example, recently decided to spend $890,265 to teach its kiddies just "how marvelous sex is." I think this is a splendidly liberal, progressive, educational idea. And I've already seized one of the opportunities by completing a much-needed new standard textbook called *Dick and Jane Find Each Other.* Naturally, I submitted it to that noted liberal, progressive educationalist Dr. Homer T. Pettibone, B.A., M.A., Phys. Ed., Director of Curriculum, Textbook Selection and Eraser Monitors. He read it with absorbed interest.

"Oh, Dick, look. Look and see. See me. See me tremble. See me tremble when I look at you."

"Oh, Jane, you have eyes. You have two eyes. They are like pools. They are like limpid pools of purple passion."

"Oh, Dick, you have arms. You have two arms. They are strong arms. Hold me in your strong arms."

"Oh, Jane, you smell. You smell good. Is that 'Nuit of Pleasure' behind your ear? I will bite. I will bite your ear."

"Oh, Dick, look. Look and see. See Spot. Spot is a dog. Dogs bark. Listen to Spot bark."

"Scram, Spot, scram. Oh, Jane, come. Come with me. Come with me behind the barn."

"Oh, Dick, oh."

"Dot, dot, dot."

"Dot, dot, dot?" said Dr. Pettibone, looking up with annoyance.

"It's only for second-graders," I explained. "Would you like to see the unexpurgated third-grade version?"

"It won't do," said Dr. Pettibone with a frown. "How do you expect any child to learn how marvelous sex is from a book like this?"

"What was good enough for their fathers," I said stoutly, "is good enough for them."

"That's an illiberal, unprogressive attitude," said Dr. Pettibone. And he went on to explain in detail exactly how all modern educationalists agree that the mysteries of sex should be taught. So I've been working on my revised, standard textbook. It begins:

"Oh, Dick, look. Look and see. See the circle on the blackboard. It is an ovary. See the ovum in the ovary? It has genes and chromosomes. It will go down that tube. That is a Fallopian tube. The Fallopian tube connects the ovary with the uterus and . . ."

I don't know how it will come out. The textbook, I mean. But if it has an honest ending Dick will say:

"Stop, Jane, stop. I am tired. I am tired of sex education. Let's go out behind the barn and play arithmetic."

—— *Is Un-American*

The State Senate's Committee on Un-American Activities has accused University of California President Clark Kerr of condoning all sorts of goings-on at Berkeley—including homosexuality, communism, LSD, sex, dirty words, rock-and-roll music, smoking marijuana and throwing up. While the report certainly raises many questions of interest to special groups—such as, "Is a coeducational institution the place for homosexuals?"—let us confine ourselves to the issue the Committee has raised that is of stimulating concern to us all:

Is sex an un-American activity?

Personally, I feel very strongly that the Un-American Activities Committee had made a dangerous leap forward by taking sex within its purview. True, it can be argued forcibly that sex is certainly not 100 per cent American. Those engaged in it, studies demonstrate, are definitely in no position to show proper respect for the flag nor, in most cases, to remove their hats for our national anthem. Moreover, it cannot be denied that it saps the will of many young ladies to resist.

On the other hand, although documentary evidence is lacking, it is widely held that at least several of our Founding Fathers themselves secretly believed in sex as a way of life. And many will argue that it is one of our cherished American heritages, handed down for one hundred and ninety years. "Where would this great nation of ours be today," they demand, "without sex?" As a moderate, however, I feel that sex is basically neither American nor un-American, but rather belongs to that gray middleground which includes lawn bowling, dandruff shampooing and fixing flat tires, the primary difference being that it is more fun.

The grave danger in declaring sex un-American, of course, is the effect this will have on our country's future. You can imagine how members of The Never Trust Anybody Over Thirty Club will react:

Jock Armstrong: How about a little un-American activities, honey?

Priscilla Primm: You mean another one of your cheap dates, like a march to legalize pot? A sit-in to overthrow the Government? A lie-in to . . . ?"

Jock: You're getting warm. I'm talking about *real* subversion.

Priscilla (half-swooning): You mean . . . Oh, Jack, I've never kissed a boy, but you make it sound so thrilling.

So, knowing our younger people, you can see the threat inherent in declaring sex subversive: a population explosion. And while I'll be the first to agree that it's most difficult to decide which activities are American and which aren't, I feel the Committee should stick to those which are less volatile, more universally decried, and in keeping with the spirit of its investigations. Like throwing up.

Faith, Charity and Edna

Once upon a time there were three beautiful sisters, Charity, Faith and Edna La Nuit. Their father's name was Horatio Alger La Nuit. On his deathbed, he gathered them around and said:

"Daughters, you must now make your own way in the world. Take stock of yourselves and set forth. But above all else, remember: To succeed in life you must be generous, honest and persevering."

With that, he breathed his last. His dutiful daughters took stock of themselves. "What," said Edna, "have we to offer?" And after a moment's thought, it was pretty obvious they had only one thing.

"I'm going to be generous," cried Charity, who was something of a do-gooder. "All I wish to do is spread happiness in the world. People want what I have. To make my fellow man happy, I am going to give it away free to one and all."

In no time, of course, she was known far and wide as a promiscuous young lady of easy virtue—in fact, a pushover.

"A nice girl like her," the neighbors all said, shaking their heads. "That's a sin."

"Daddy was wrong about generosity," said Faith, a more hard-headed type. "Honesty is clearly the key. This is the land of individual liberty and the great enterprise system. People don't want something for nothing. They want what they have to pay for. Therefore, I must go forth and honestly sell myself to the world in a forthright business manner."

In no time, of course, she was doing six months in the pokey. "A nice girl like her," the neighbors all said, shaking their heads. "That's a crime."

This left Edna, who was the smartest of the three. "If it isn't generosity," she said, "and if it isn't honesty, it must be perseverance. I shall go forth and persevere."

So she got a job as a topless waitress. And persevered. This got her a shot in the chorus line. Where she persevered. Eventually, she was spotted by a Hollywood casting director, who, after several lengthy interviews, announced to the press: "I have decided to give Miss La Nuit the leading role in *Sexpots Aboil*, as she is a young lady of great promise. And, off the record, fellas," muttered the casting director, "one of these nights she better keep it."

But Edna persevered. In no time, she was a star of stage, screen and television. She married three millionaires, made the cover of *Fortune*, the best-dressed list and the White House Festival of the Arts. "The secret of my success is perseverance," Edna always told interviewers. "Or, to put it another way, people want what they can't have."

Her rags-to-riches story warmed everyone's heart. "A nice

girl like her," said the neighbors, shaking their heads in admiration. "That's America."

Moral: Love's funny. You can't sell it and you can't give it away. But keep it, and you'll get a good deal.

Belt Chastity

Grave concern is being voiced over the growing problem of sex on our college campuses. Magazine cover stories, books such as *Sex and the College Girl,* learned papers by sociologists—all emphasize the emotional havoc this trend is wreaking on our immature coeds. No rational person could disagree. Do you realize that, despite this increasing sexual affluence, thousands of our young women go through college without a single pass being made at them? The high cost to the Nation in wounded egos, latent neuroses and feelings of rejection is incalculable. There is no question these pockets of sexual deprivation must be wiped out.

The case for an all-out war on sexual poverty has never been better stated, I feel, than in a recent letter to *The New Republic,* an erudite, liberal journal. It was from a Mr. Burling Lowrey of Washington, D.C. And he demands a Federal crash program and cites as his authority "a little-known book, *The Sexually Deprived: A National Disgrace,* by Professor Orber Rebro."

This crash program, as Mr. Lowrey envisions it, would include: "(1) mass psychoanalysis for cases of insufferable repression; (2) implementation of the 'Harvard Plan' by busing coeds in order to break up patterns of *de facto* segregation; and (3) revival of the 'Personals' column in *The Saturday Review*." In a veritable trumpet call for action now, Mr. Lowrey concludes: "Not until *all* of our college students enjoy the benefits of sexual affluence will our nation be strong and free."

While the problem is admittedly serious and while few can argue with Mr. Lowrey's goal of equal opportunity for all, I feel however that his demand for a crash program illustrates the unusual Pavlovian response of liberals to any crisis: Let Washington handle it. But what, actually, would such a massive program entail? First, it would mean the appointment of a federal Sex Czar, probably Mr. Shriver. Next would come a proliferation of costly new agencies and projects, such as a Youth Consolation Corps, a Domestic Dance Corps, Corsage Subsidies and long-term grants for the redevelopment of blighted coeds. All of which would instill in our young ladies a "something for nothing" philosophy. Worse, federal aid means federal controls. Do we want our deprived coeds subjected to snooping social workers, activity reports in triplicate and a degrading "means test"?

No! I say, and I'm sure Ronald Reagan would agree, that the reason so many of our coeds are deprived is that they think deprived. What they need are the qualities that made America great: Confidence, drive, self-reliance and tighter sweaters.

Can faraway Washington bureaucrats meet these needs? Nonsense. The war on sexual poverty can best be won by vigorous voluntary action at the community level. Enlist now. With charity in your heart, visit your local sorority house. Wink at the wallflowers. Flirt with the repressed. Take a shy girl to lunch. Remember that "Today's Coeds Are Tomorrow's Mothers."

But, of course, that's another problem. And I, for one, am perfectly willing to let Washington worry about that.

Creeping Sexicare

Herewith are another two chapters in that standard un-published reference book *A History of the World, 1950–1999*. The titles of these unprinted chapters are, "The Advent of Socialized Sin" and "Meeting the Unmet Needs."

I.

It was in the late 1960s that the Great Society made a magnificent leap forward to realize one of mankind's age-old dreams—legalized prostitution. Long advocated by liberals, feminists and assorted sociologists, this progressive social change met strong opposition from hidebound conservatives. Their protests led to the famed March for Free Enterprise, in which 5000 young ladies paraded down Pennsylvania Avenue waving placards saying: "NO GOVERNMENT CONTROLS!" "INDIVIDUAL INITIATIVE MADE THIS COUNTRY GREAT," "NO FEE SCHEDULES!" "DON'T DESTROY

THE SACRED PRACTITIONER-PATIENT RELATIONSHIP" and "HEAVEN HELP US WORKING GIRLS."

The President met them with the ringing words, "Ask not what your country can do for you . . ." And the measure finally passed Congress. Now that the profession was legal, a bitter dispute arose in Washington as to which Government agency should control it. Parks and Recreation; Health, Education and Welfare; the Department of Natural Resources; and the Bureau of Wildlife Management all claimed jurisdiction. At last, the President created a new agency, The Office of Vice Control, to direct what he called "The War on Promiscuity." Corporal Shriver (no relation) was named to run it. As a first step, all young ladies of the evening were required to obtain licenses, issued only after rigorous written examinations administered, in most states, by the Department of Motor Vehicles.

With the help of the Bureau of Vocational Standards and the Department of Labor, services were standardized and federal minimum wages of sin established. A vast building program resulted in a new Government building in each postal zone, complete with flag, flagpole and the words chiseled into its concrete façade: "UNITED STATES GOVERNMENT BORDELLO." Inside, each boasted gleaming linoleum floors, bright fluorescent lights, pictures of the President and George Washington on the walls, and a clerk ready to help the public fill the necessary application forms and direct them to their physical examinations and supervised showers. At the exit a trained social worker waited to compile valuable data for official studies and surveys through interviews in depth.

After the initial year of operation, Corporal Shriver reported proudly to the President on the program's unqualified success.

"For the first time in the history of mankind, sir," he said, "we have put sin on a clean, orderly and superbly efficient basis."

"A triumph," said the President, well-pleased. "And how do the customers like it?"

"You know, it's odd, sir," said Corporal Shriver, frowning. "But we haven't had one yet."

II.

In the United States, the presidential election of 1976 shaped up as another traditional battle between the Democrats and Republicans. The Democrats, as usual, pointed with pride to such programs as Medicare, Denticare, Judicare, Menticare, Pedicare and Opti-Auri-Nasicare and said they had "met the needs of the people." The Republicans, as usual, retorted angrily that they, too, were for these programs, were for meeting the needs of the people and were also for economy in government. Many voters saw little to choose, and pollsters, with a yawn, rated the election a toss-up.

It was at this point that Mr. Rock Hunter, a middle-aged motion-picture star, announced his candidacy and unveiled a new program that was to arouse America as nothing ever had before.

"It is true," said Mr. Hunter at a dramatic press conference, "that the welfare state now assures that each of us gets enough medicine, enough dentistry, enough legal aid, enough mental health and enough arch support. But what of those of us who, through no fault of our own, haven't been getting enough lately?"

"Enough what?" asked a puzzled reporter.

Mr. Hunter smiled his famous warm and friendly smile. "Love," he said, simply. And with that was launched the greatest welfare program of them all—Sexicare!

"Do you realize," thundered Mr. Hunter in speeches from coast to coast, "that two-thirds of our nation goes to bed each night ill-content, underloved and alone? Surely, a government as prosperous as ours can take care of those who are romantically disadvantaged, emotionally deprived and sexually underprivileged."

Sexicare immediately struck a chord in America's heart. With every citizen inculcated from infancy by sexy movies, sexy books and sexy commercials, it fulfilled the greatest unmet need of all. True, there was scattered opposition. The concept of more sex was opposed by a coalition of Southern Baptists and Playboy Bunnies, though perhaps for different reasons. And the anarchist-oriented Sexual Freedom League split down the middle, some being for sex and some for freedom. But Mr. Hunter was elected in a landslide. At his inauguration he swore to "set a glorious example for every American." Unfortunately, he died three weeks after taking office—his last words being "enough is enough." He was replaced by the Vice-President, a dour New England parson of eighty-three who had been selected to balance the ticket.

He promptly abolished Sexicare, along with miniskirts, mascara and drive-in movies. Sex once again became illicit.

Oddly enough, there was little protest. As a Young Socialist League recruiter confessed after being caught chasing three Vassar girls through Central Park: "The welfare state may fill man's needs, but individual initiative is sure lots more fun."

One Big Family

We've Been Stung

It was with horror and amazement that I stumbled across statistics the other day proving that White Anglo-Saxon Protestants—or "WASPs," as they are called—are definitely a minority group. And a minor one at that. True, there are fewer Jews in this country than WASPs, but there are probably as many Negroes and far more Catholics. This is shocking.

What is shocking, of course, is that in the entire history of our great land no one has thought to organize a systematic campaign of persecution against the WASPs. Is this equality? Is this democracy? Is this fair play? Obviously not. To rectify this grievous oversight, I am immediately organizing the Klique Klaque Klan. Membership is strictly limited to Jews, Negroes, Catholics, Fabian Socialists, Rosicrucians and all other true Americans. Our dogma is set forth in that ancient, well-authenticated manuscript I am now busy writing called *The Secret Protocols of the Elders of Madison Avenue*.

This irrefutable work traces the insidious WASP conspiracy in this country back to the landing of the Pilgrims —each and every one of whom was a dedicated WASP agent. Thanks to their spadework, the WASP plotters were able to seize control at the very founding of our Government. Merely read the list of those who signed the Declaration of Independence. WASP names all. Is it any wonder the WASP-dominated Continental Congress gave command to that well-known WASP George Washington? Yes, the very George Washington who is recognized today as "The Father of the WASP Cabal." Nor can it be denied that the clever Wasps have run this nation ever since. Virtually every president had been a Wasp. And the few exceptions—Van Buren, both Roosevelts, Eisenhower and Kennedy—have found themselves surrounded by WASP advisers in the White House, which has long been a veritable WASPs' nest. Not only have WASPs infiltrated all branches of government but they have clearly taken over Wall Street. Look at the biggest brokerage house. Merrill, Lynch, Pierce, Fenner & Smith all have a WASPish ring.

Worse, they have seized control of our mass media. Would anyone contest that Batten, Barton, Durstine & (undoubtedly) Osborn aren't predominantly WASPs? No wonder our television heroes, our advertising models—our very image of an American—look like WASPs. Citizens, we are being brainwashed! Unquestionably, then, this minority group is now in control of our politics, our finances and our minds. To whom do they owe their allegiance? Us or Mother England? Us or the National Council of Churches? Would you want your sister to marry a pasty-faced WASP?

Arise, fellow members of the Klique Klaque Klan. Cut eye-slits in your checkered tablecloths. Burn a Star of David on your neighbor's lawn. Squash a WASP today. For how can our nation ever be a true melting pot of all races, colors and creeds until we've heaved everybody in?

A Dead Issue

A grave problem has arisen in the South. The Defense Department is cancelling all contracts with private undertakers who refuse to handle the bodies of Negro servicemen. And the White undertakers are tearing up their lucrative Government contracts. Who ever heard of such an undertaking by undertakers?

In puzzlement, I called on my friend, Colonel Jefferson Davis Stonewall, bereavement director of The Eternal Rest (for Whites only) Funeral Parlor.

Q—Colonel, about segregated funeral establishments . . .

A—Now hold on, son. We Southerners love our Nigras. But we got to preserve the purity of our White race.

Q—I know how you Southerners feel about miscegenation, Colonel. But when a Negro's dead . . .

A—Look here, son. Just ask yourself. You want your sister to marry a dead Nigra?

Q—Your feelings do run deep, indeed, Colonel. But in this case the dead Negroes are servicemen, presumably men who have joined the Army to help defend our American heritage of equal rights for all.

A—Oh, we cotton to that, son. Yes sir, the White soldier should be out there fighting for his equal rights and the Colored boy should be out there fighting for his equal rights, too. We Southerners believe in equal rights, four-square.

Q—You do?

A—That's right, son. Separate but equal rights.

Q—Separate but equal rights?

A—It's the heart of our Southern culture, son. Our Nigras got the same right to eat at a Colored lunch counter as we got to eat at a White one. We give them the equal right to live separately, die separately and be buried separately. In a separate but equal plot. Whether they like it or not.

Q—But I still don't see what harm a Negro can do you when he's dead, Colonel.

A—What harm! You take the present case. Who's stirring up all the fuss? Dead Nigras.

Q—But they're servicemen, stationed down here to . . .

A—That's right! Most of them's uppity Northern Nigras. Outside racial agitators, that's what they are!

Q—But, Colonel, they . . .

A—Undoubtedly Commie inspired!

Q—But, Colonel . . .

A—Aiming at overthrowing our traditional Southern way of death! With the help of that interfering Federal Government!

Q—But . . .

A—Staging lying-down demonstrations in our sacred Southern homes of eternal peace! Going limp! You can't even stir them with an electric prod! They got no respect for the dead!

Q—But, Colonel, they are dead.

A—Don't make no never mind. We know all about these uppity Nigras who are dying for integration. And in the South, son, even that won't do them no good.

Colonel Stonewall's Reward

(Scene: A magnolia-scented path leading to a pearly gate. Colonel Jefferson Lee Stonewall approaches, somewhat nervously. Waiting to greet him is The Gatekeeper, who wears a khaki uniform, badge and white helmet.)

The Gatekeeper (smiling): Now don't you fret, Colonel. You're not going to have no trouble getting in here.

The Colonel (with annoyance): That problem, sir, didn't so much as flicker across my mind. Why, I've been a decent Southern Christian gentleman all my born days. Went to my Southern Christian Church every Sunday and, like the Bible says, I loved my fellow man. Excepting, of course, for outside agitators, Republicans and uppity Nigras.

The Gatekeeper: Of course.

The Colonel (*removing his straw hat to mop his brow*): But, tell the truth, I'm a mite worried about what kind of folks you got inside this place.

The Gatekeeper: What kind of folks?

The Colonel (*hesitantly*): Well, I'm not criticizing, mind you. But the Bible's just a trifle hazy on the point. It keeps saying all us decent Christian folks are going to dwell together throughout eternity. But it don't precisely spell out what kind of folks.

The Gatekeeper: You mean?

The Colonel (*in a rush*): I mean, Am I going to have to dwell throughout eternity with a bunch of Nigras?

The Gatekeeper (*shocked*): Why, Colonel, whatever did put such an idea in your head? You know they never were allowed in our many fine Southern Christian Churches. You think they're going to be allowed in here?

The Colonel (*with an immense sigh of relief*): Praise the Lord, who, as we used to say in church, wouldn't have created two separate races if he didn't believe in segregation.

The Gatekeeper: That's right, Colonel. It's the way you reckoned it ought to be. You just walk in through those pearly gates marked "White Only." And the Colored folk, they got their own separate-but-almost-equal facility down over there across the tracks. No intermingling. You'll never see a Nigra again.

The Colonel (*happily*): I knew it all the time. Only you ought to find some way of letting folks know back on earth. It sure would ease a lot of nagging worries.

The Gatekeeper (*smiling*): They just got to have faith.

ACT II

(*Scene: a magnolia-scented pink cloud, six weeks later. The Colonel sits, moodily sipping a mint nectar. He looks awful.*)

The Gatekeeper (*passing by*): Enjoying yourself, Colonel?

The Colonel: Tell the truth, I'm not. Oh, there's plenty of everything. But there's nobody to serve it with a respectful smile. There's nobody sitting on the back of the cloud. When I holler "Boy!" nobody comes. How can a man feel naturally superior when there's nobody around to feel superior to?

The Gatekeeper: Well, like I said, there's no Nigras here.

The Colonel: You mean I got to go through eternity feeling like this? (*snorting*) And you call this heaven!

The Gatekeeper (*surprised*): Heaven? I thought you knew, Colonel. This is hell.

Our Alienable Rights

It's certainly heartwarming to see the way everybody's fighting for our rights these days. The Realtors are fighting for our property rights. And the Negroes are fighting for our equal rights. And naturally they are most fighting each other. What they're fighting about, as you know, is the Rumford Fair-Housing Law. Which says you can't refuse to rent an apartment to a Negro solely because he's a Negro. No sir, you have to think up another reason not to rent an apartment to him. The Realtors say this will destroy our property rights. "The Government," they say, "can't tell a man what to do with his property. He's got an inalienable right to do with it as he pleases." And I was so tickled to hear this that I hustled next door to enlist Mr. Cogswell's support for my hot-dog stand.

"Hot-dog stand!" says Mr. Cogswell, who happens to be a Realtor and very strong on property rights.

"You bet," says I. "It'll be red, white and blue with revolving neon signs and it'll dress up my front yard. Not to mention turning it into a money-making proposition."

"Hold it," says he. "This neighborhood is zoned R-1, and it would violate the set-back ordinance, the Health Code, the . . ."

"Right," says I, "and we must work together to repeal these unwarranted interferences with my inalienable property rights."

"Moreover," says he, "it would ruin property values and create a traffic problem. Where, for example, would you park your beat-up old car?"

"On your lawn," says I. "My car may be old and beat-up, but it's mine. And I will do with it as I please."

"And I will have the law on you," says he, "for trespassing, illegal parking and felony mopery."

"What about my property rights?" says I. "We must abolish these laws telling me what I can and can't do with my very own house and my very own car."

"What are you," says he, "some kind of nut?"

"Your father's mustache," says I.

"With bells on," says he.

So I march into my house to get my very own meat cleaver to do with as I please. And he picks up his very own hedge clippers, intending to do with them as he pleases. And if the cops hadn't come along and infringed on our inalienable property rights through confiscation, there's no doubt one of us would have lost his head.

Well, it just shows you the whole trouble with inalienable rights. They keep alienating everybody. My property rights interfere with Mr. Cogswell's property rights. And his with mine. And, above all, somebody's property rights are always fouling up somebody else's human rights. Personally, I think we ought to settle for just one right: the right to do what we please with our lives and our property—as long as we don't hurt somebody else. Neither his person, his property nor his feelings. And the prime function of government is to see that we don't. You know, like by enforcing the Rumford Law.

Share the Klan

Ah, what a lovely world. Everybody wants to share equally with everybody else. Poor young radicals want to share the wealth; rich old conservatives want to share the taxes; and Senator Russell of Georgia wants to share the Negroes. The Senator's very serious. He says Mississippi's population is 42 percent Negro. But Vermont's is only one tenth of 1 percent. He says this isn't fair and he wants the Federal

Government to divvy up Negroes equally until every state's got 10.5 percent. This, he says, would cost $1.5 billion. Which sounds very serious to me.

Well, I'm sure this Share-the-Negro Plan is most generous of the Senator. But you can see where it's going to lead. Southern Negroes are going to counter with a Share-the-Bigot proposal. I can hear their leaders now: "Do you realize that 58 percent of Mississippi's population believes in white supremacy? While up in Vermont it's only one tenth of 1 percent. Is this fair? We demand that every state be given its quota of 10.5 percent white supremacists!"

Oh, what a black day for our beloved Northern way of life! As the scion of an old Northern antebellum World War II) family, I can only shudder to think of our fair North being flooded with banjo-playing Mississippi demagogues, fat Alabama police chiefs and red-necked Georgia crackers. I ask you, fellow Northerners, do you want a Georgia cracker living next door to you? Going around in a white sheet, burning crosses and otherwise lowering property values? Worst of all, do you want your sister to marry a cracker? What a crummy thought!

And think what would happen if these Southern carpetbaggers gained control of our state government and imposed their alien philosophies on us. Right away, we'd have to double the number of our rest rooms, schools, swimming pools and drinking fountains. The expense alone would ruin taxpayers. Can you imagine enforcing such customs as making our Negro citizens move to the back of the bus? Have you ever tried to move to the back of a Northern bus? We'd have a race riot on every bus every peak hour. Instead of just the regular riots we have now. Oh, I know we Northerners have problems in the field of civil rights. But I say, let us solve them in our own fashion. The last thing we need is for the ever encroaching Federal Government to force a lot of Southern bigots on us to preach their doctrine of white supremacy, stirring up trouble, fear and hate. Stand up for our state's rights! We must fight, fellow Northerners, to preserve our Northern way of life, to defend Northern womanhood, to . . . .

Excuse me. I guess you think I'm getting carried away. I know Senator Russell only suggested sending us Negroes. And not those terrrible white supremacists. But I figure when a man wants to share with you that bad, what he really wants to share are his problems.

And I can't see there's any question which group's causing all the problems.

Them and Me

Everyone is dissecting the race riots. The conservatives are blaming the liberals, the liberals are blaming the bigots, the bigots are smiling smugly. The insurance companies are worried about claims, the politicians about re-election. And the editorial writers are urging more respect for law and order. The sociologists are talking of "lack of economic opportunity," the psychiatrists of "frustrations." The civil rights workers are shaking their heads and saying the cause of equality under the law has suffered "a severe setback."

Yet all I can think of is they wanted to kill me. The uneasiness grew slowly. The first day it seemed just another riot. A shame. But these things will happen. Then came the next day. And the next. At first, I tried to imagine how the rioters felt, smashing and burning. I thought I could sense how a young Negro boy must feel as he heaved a rock through a plate-glass window. The release. The rebellion without hope of success. The simple act of saying to hell with a world you could never conquer. It was an act, really, of complete defeat. How terribly sad that was.

Then, slowly, as story followed story, the thread of hatred broadened. "Get Whitey! Kill him! Kill, kill, kill!" And picture followed picture. The sullen faces, the narrowed eyes. The hatred. Slowly I came to understand that they wanted to kill *me*. Quite literally, if they could only lay their hands on me, they would relish shooting me, stabbing me or beating me to death. Quite literally, paranoiac though it may sound, they wanted to kill me. They hated Me.

Suddenly it was no longer a deprived minority rebelling against the system that oppressed them. Suddenly the whole thing descended to a far more basic level—They and I, Them and Me. If They in Los Angeles and Newark and Detroit hated me, what about They who live in our own ghettos? Those near my own house? What about the bootblack? We've always gotten along so well, kidding and joshing. Does he seem a little surly this morning? What of the cleaning lady I like so well? Is there a new touch of defiance in her tone? And what of the big longshoreman coming my way down the street? What is that look in his eyes? What are They really thinking? How much do They hate Me? How awful it is to be hated. How unfair. I keep wanting to say, Don't hate me. If you must hate, hate the Thurmonds, the Eastlands, the Wallaces. Hate those who won't rent you a room or serve you a meal or give you a job. But don't hate me. I don't want it to be Them and Me. We are all fellow human beings. We are all in the same boat. Don't hate me.

In the end, I told a long-time Negro friend (I think he is a friend) of my fear and anger. I told him how awful it was to be hated. How insecure it made you, never to be sure what They were thinking. How terribly, terribly unfair it was to be despised, not for anything you'd said, or done, or been. But simply because you were white.

"I know how it is," he said, nodding. "Simply because I'm black."

Horatio Finds Friendship

Once upon a time there was a young Negro lad named Horatio Alger who, despite his humble origins, was determined to persevere.

"In this great land of ours," he would earnestly tell his school chums in the ghetto, "any poor boy can grow up to be rich, successful and respected."

"Man, you're out of your skull," his little friends would reply. "Let's go steal hubcaps."

But young Horatio persevered. He eschewed bad companions. He devoted every waking moment to reading worthwhile books, doing isometric exercises and slaving diligently at honest employment. By the time he had put himself through college he was superbly conditioned, brilliantly educated and possessed of the highest moral character, marked by an indomitable will to persevere. He got a job in a bank which desperately needed to hire one Negro in order to escape prosecution under the fair employment laws. Horatio persevered. He married a lovely girl, had a lovely son, rose through incredible efforts to a vice-presidency and at last achieved his lifelong dream: a $75,000 house in the suburbs with radio-controlled garage doors and an automatic sprinkler system.

The riots lasted five days.

After the welcome died down, Horatio wiped the rotten eggs off his suit, replaced the broken windows of his new home and told his little family: "Don't worry, we have some bad neighbors and some good neighbors. But if we persevere, all the neighbors will come to treat us equally."

And this came true. The bad neighbors (53.2 percent) never smiled at the Algers. The good neighbors (46.8 percent) smiled overly profusely. But all the neighbors (100 percent) wouldn't let their daughters go dancing with Horatio's son. So while Horatio was rich and successful, he didn't feel respected somehow in White middle-class society. In fact, he felt downright lonely.

"At least," he said to himself, "I have won the respect of my own people by the splendid example I have set in becoming rich and successful." And he went back to the ghetto to enjoy it.

"Persevere, friends," Horatio told his old down-and-out

school chums, "and you can all become rich and successful like me."

After he had wiped the rotten eggs off his suit (and had his head bandaged for a nasty wound caused by a flying brick), Horatio decided on the only possible course: He sold his home with the automatic sprinkler system and his two cars and his gray flannel suit, gave the money to S.N.C.C., moved back to the ghetto, went on relief and became a leading advocate of Black Power.

"You're a born troublemaker, Alger," a social worker told him after his third arrest for inciting to riot. "If you had only persevered, just think where you'd be today."

Horatio sighed. "Without a friend in the world," he said.

Moral: In this great land of ours any young Negro lad can grow up to be rich and successful. If he isn't lucky.

The American Way

The True Follower

Q—Good evening, sir. Congratulations on winning the True American Award for 1965. Would you mind stepping over here and saying a few words for our television audience?

A—Not at all. Thank you very much. It's a high honor. But a lot of the credit should go to my wife here and all the other members of my family for supporting my basic stand on the issues of the day.

Q—And what is your stand, sir?

A—Well, we like to think of it as loyalty. We say that if true Americans don't have loyalty to, respect for and confidence in the high officials in charge of running our government, then our democracy's in pretty bad shape.

Q—I see. And how do you, as a true American, go about demonstrating your loyalty to these officials?

A—We do wish you wouldn't use the word "demonstrating." It suggests marches and sit-ins and things. We feel that, at the very least, these demonstrations show a lack of confidence in what our leaders are doing.

Q—That does seem true.

A—Of course, we don't just sit back and do nothing. For one thing, we write angry letters to the editor deploring those who take stands we disagree with.

Q—Such as?

A—Well, primarily we deplore those who deplore what our leaders are doing. Now we don't say these people are disloyal. After all, it's a free country. But certainly all this carping criticism doesn't help any. We must all pull together behind our leaders if they are to solve the grave crises we face.

Q—What crisis do you consider the gravest?

A—Oh, Vietnam, without question. There's not the slightest doubt our President has to put up with more criticism on what he's doing in Vietnam than on any other issue.

Q—As a true American, I take it you approve of what the President is doing there?

A—Of course. It's a typical case of a vocal minority voicing unreasoning criticism. Take the President's decision to widen the war by bombing North Vietnam. Its perfectly clear that very few Americans understand why he's doing it. Yet they criticize him for it!

Q—A questionable attitude.

A—It certainly is. For obviously, the President has reasons for doing what he's doing. Therefore, he must know something we don't know. Yet these naggers of little faith, without having all the facts, contend that what he's doing is immoral, illegal and highly dangerous. Well, I'm sure I speak for every true American when I say I hope the President won't be deterred by such disrespectful disloyalty from continuing to do what he's doing. Whatever that may be.

Q—Thank you, sir. Congratulations again. And could we have your name for the viewing public?

A—Yes, it's Lemming. George C. Lemming. This is Mrs. Lemming. And let me just say again that when it comes to having unquestioning faith that our leaders are leading us in the right direction, you can always count on us Lemmings.

The Three R's

The trustees and directors take pride in announcing the opening next fall of the new Uriah P. Fagin School for Boys and Girls. Its motto: *"Caveat Emptor."* The philosophy behind the Fagin School was best summed up by its headmaster, Dr. T. Homer Pettibone, Ph.D., Ed.D., Ls.D.:

"The duty of an educational system is (1) to inculcate in the student the goals of his society and (2) to equip him to meet its challenges. Our present system fails dismally.

"It is thus our high hope at the new Fagin School to matriculate young men and women adequately prepared to (1) make a fast buck and (2) not get caught."

Dr. Pettibone, himself, will teach the basic philosophy course, "From Attila the Hun to Modern Corporate Ethics."

Required reading includes Machiavelli, Nietzsche and the Truth in Advertising Code. Courses in the New Math will concentrate on the preparation of income-tax forms, with special emphasis on legitimate business deductions which cannot be double-checked. Originally, the New Math was to have covered the preparation of expense accounts as well. But it was felt this subject could better be dealt with in our Creative Writing Department. In our well-equipped chemistry laboratory, students will conduct experiments which will teach them to make lysergic acid, mescaline, peyote, the dry martini and other aids to making our cities more livable. Other science courses include, "Bugs and How To Wire Them."

In public speaking, the students will learn how to speak extemporaneously on any subject for a full hour without saying anything. This is only one of the many courses in the field of American government, which offers so many career opportunities for promising Fagin School graduates. Examinations will, of course, be conducted on the honor system, with proctors monitoring secretly through one-way glass mirrors. As in other schools, higher grades will be awarded for successful cheating. In addition, however, subtle bribery and polite extortion will be encouraged to bring out the student's best in his relationship with his teacher.

While the academic is stressed, the body is not forgotten. Advanced young ladies will be given a full course in the modern dance. (Students must bring their own topless bikinis.) And the physical education program for young men will be under the direction of Mr. William (Brick Wall) Ngckyschwxski, the noted professional football player. He will lecture from personal experience on "The Key to Remaining Physically Fit Between 18½ and 25—a Trick Knee." Or, as Dr. Pettibone put it, *"Mens sana in corpore 4-F."*

Tuition is $3500 per annum in unmarked bills. While this may seem exorbitant, it must be remembered that we parents set the goals and challenges of our modern society, and thus we owe our children the education necessary to meet them successfully.

Or, as Dr. Pettibone expresses it so well: "A year in the Fagin School now may well save ten in Leavenworth later."

Sing It Right

One of our Republican senators has been poking fun at the Right Wing for demanding a Congressional investigation of folk songs. On the grounds, says the Right Wing, that these "hootenannies have been used to brainwash and subvert" us all. The Senator is making speeches about "Mine Enemy, the Folk Singer." Which is very funny and all that. But, personally, I think the Right Wing's right. Do you want to be brainwashed by a hootenanny? It's enough to give you nightmares. Moreover, the most authentic old folk songs are laments about love and peace and that sort of thing. Issues which definitely smack of Left Wing tendencies these days.

Is this fair? Of course not. What our nation needs, so that we can be brainwashed equally by both sides, are more

Right Wing folk songs. I've been working on it, and we now have plans for a Superpatriotic Hootenanny in the Hollywood Bowl starring the Slimefighters, a dashing quartet composed of a Young American for Freedom, two chiropractors wearing steel-rimmed glasses, and a little old lady in tennis shoes. Who sings bass. To warm up the crowd, the program will open with one of those typical love songs you hear at hootenannies. You know, the girl is torn trying to choose between two swains. The lights will go down, the three men will hum mournfully into their kazoos, and the little old lady will clutch the microphone to croon that sad ballad: "I've Got Two Loves, Quemoy and Matsu."

With that, the quartet will swing into a foot-tapping rendition of "There's Something Foreign About Earl Warren," followed by one of those true folk tributes to a true folk hero: "Oh, My Darling Robert Welch (The Marxist-Leninists You Will Squelch)." Then we'll have a brief intermission to give members of the audience time to pass their tracts, brochures and impeachment petitions among themselves. The lights will dim once more and we will hear the plaintive strains of that Old English lament: "Where Have All the Skybolts Gone?" With a counterpoint of "We'll Hang McNamara From a Sour Apple Tree." When the applause and calls for a lynching have died down, the quartet's voices will swell into the stirring grand finale: "I've Got an H-Bomb." Which goes: "And I'm going to bomb for victory, all over this world . . ." Oh, there won't be a bloodless eye in the house.

Of course, the purists will sniff at our hootenanny. They'll say these old folk songs we made up aren't authentic. But what can we do? Very few authentic old folk songs have militant Right Wing messages. I guess it's that the plain people who make up folk songs would rather sing yearningly about love and peace than militantly about hate and war. But, after all, they've been doing it for a couple of hundred years. I say let's give the other side a chance.

Rally 'Round the Flag

The National Committee To Show Our Flag has entered the controversy between the Daughters of the American Revolution and the Treo Company, Inc., makers of the "Stars 'n' Stripes" panty girdle. As you may have read, the good ladies of the D.A.R. complained the undergarment was "a shocking caricature" of the American flag. Mr. Harry L. Gross of Treo, who must have felt somewhat like Stonewall Jackson marching into Fredericktown, promptly withdrew. That is, he withdrew all 3000 Stars 'n' Stripes from the market.

"We will burn the damn things or send them to some foreign country where our flag isn't involved," he said. "Maybe we can give them away as charity gifts to people in other parts of the world."

It was at this point, of course, that The National Committee To Show Our Flag stepped in. In a statement to the press, the Committee's Honorary Chairman, Corporal Homer T. Pettibone, U. S. Army Flying Corps (retired), said he was "deeply moved by Mr. Gross's patriotic offer."

"Let me begin," said Corporal Pettibone, fingering the Good Conduct ribbon in the lapel of his conservative blue suit, "by saying that we do not agree with the D.A.R. that this garment is a shocking caricature of our flag. True, it has only seven stars round the waistband, but our investigation shows the legs display the requisite thirteen red-and-white stripes. At least in the larger sizes. It was the general conclusion of our committee, therefore, that a lump would rise in the throat of any patriotic man to see the Stars 'n' Stripes passing by. As we constantly emphasize, no one can wave the flag too much. On the other hand, the Committee did foresee grave problems involving flag etiquette. The requirement that men remove their hats and servicemen must salute when Old Glory passes would, we felt, cause considerable confusion. Particularly in downtown areas on windy days. There was also the difficulty of suitable ceremonies at sunset and the seemingly insuperable problem of observing proper flag etiquette on days of national mourning.

"Thus, in the final analysis, the Committee wholeheartedly applauds Mr. Gross's decision to send the Stars 'n' Stripes abroad. It is in keeping with our spirit of Manifest Destiny. It is a vibrant echo of Teddy Roosevelt's Great White Fleet. As befits a world power, we shall show our flag in every foreign clime. And brave hearts everywhere, gentlemen, shall leap up. Moreover, the Committee feels it can count on the strong support of President Johnson for this people-to-people aid program to overdeveloped countries. For he never spoke truer words than during the height of the

Dominican crisis when he recited from memory a passage he had learned in a recitation contest as a little boy:

"'I have seen the glories of art and architecture, and mountain and river; I have seen the sunset on the Jungfrau, and the full moon rise over Mont Blanc. But the fairest vision on which these eyes ever looked was the flag of my country in a foreign land.'"

The Super Revolution

Like many great changes in history, the Second American Revolution was triggered by a seemingly inauspicious event: Mr. Herbert C. Cogshaw's wife sent him to the store to buy a box of dog biscuits.

"A jumbo-sized box of giant-sized biscuits," he muttered to himself with a frown of concentration. "A jumbo-sized box . . ."

After an hour's hunt, he finally settled for a giant-sized box of jumbo-sized biscuits and presented it to the checker, a bored young lady in a Mickey Mouse costume.

"Thank you, sir," she said, putting it in a bag. "And here's your set of Indian earthenware potholders."

"No, thank you," said Mr. Cogshaw. "I just want a box of dog biscuits."

"The potholders are free today," explained the young lady. "And here's your Purple Pleasure Stamps, your entry blank for the Fun in Des Moines Weekend, your Super-

Keen-O Card, your Cash-on-the-Barrelhead barrel and ten
free tickets to the Bach Topless Review Festival."

"All I want," said Mr. Cogshaw, firmly, "is a box of dog
biscuits."

"Now I'll just spin the Lucky Loop-O Wheel for you,"
said the bored young lady.

"I don't gamble," said Mr. Cogshaw irritably. "Please
give me my dog biscuits."

The wheel clacked to a stop on Triple Catharsis! Just
as the Lucky Lavender Light went on! Precisely at the
moment the Krazy Koo-koo Bird emerged! Rockets burst
into the air as a brass band struck up "God Bless America."

"You've won!" cried the store manager, rushing up happily to shake Mr. Cogshaw's hand. "The photographers are
on their way. My store will be famous. Now, are you going
to choose the Trip to Outer Mongolia for a Family of Seven
or the Free Lifetime Ping-Pong Lessons?"

"All I want," said Mr. Cogshaw plaintively, "is a box
of dog biscuits."

"Come, come," said the manager, frowning. "Let's not
be un-American. You've won the Lucky Loop-O Super
Prize. Please say, 'Gosh, I can't believe it!' Or some similar
phrase."

That was when something inside Mr. Cogshaw's mind
snapped. Shouting "Sanity Forever!" he raged through the
store, destroying entry blanks, coupons, trading stamps and
everything labeled "Jumbo." It took four policemen to carry
him off to jail. The story was a nationwide sensation. And
when Mr. Cogshaw noted mildly at his trial that the con-
sumer paid for all prizes and bonuses, he touched a chord

in the country's breast. Housewives began refusing to enter contests or to accept coupons or stamps. Angry mobs, crying "Sanity Forever!" tore down free parking lots and burned all disposable products. The economy collapsed, the Government fell and a new President was elected on the platform: "Sanity Forever—You Can't Get Something for Nothing!"

Mr. Cogshaw, a national hero, was released from jail and brought to the White House.

"Mr. Cogshaw, you have restored American integrity," said the President, shaking his hand. "In return, what can a greatful nation bestow?"

And, oh, the cheer that went up when Mr. Cogshaw replied with honesty and dignity:

"All I want, sir, is a big box of big dog biscuits."

Respect Life or We'll Kill You

One of the most burning moral issues of our time is capital punishment. And after carefully weighing the arguments on both sides, I'd like to say a few words about the death penalty: It isn't enough.

The purpose of the death penalty, everybody agrees, is to show killers that killing people is bad. Which we do by killing them. And that sure shows them. But is this example effective on potential killers? Not very. Because no matter how many people we kill to show people that killing people is bad, people still go on killing people. Obviously then, the death penalty alone isn't a strong enough deterrent. And after much thought, I have formed the Bring Back the Rack Committee, a do-good organization.

Our platform calls for abolishing the ineffective gas chamber and installing up-to-date Medieval racks in every death cell. Along with lashes, flails, thumb screws and Iron Maidens. With proper know-how, an execution might well last several weeks. Equally important, of course, is to reverse our present incomprehensible policy prohibiting photographs of the execution itself. What good is a deterrent like killing people if the public doesn't know exactly how we do it? That's the whole purpose of capital punishment.

So our Committee is suggesting that once the new devices are installed, a daily report on the progress of each execution be made to the public via television. Perhaps we might look in each evening after the Popeye show. In order to reach potential killers in the most impressionable age group. Radio listeners, of course, would have to be satisfied with merely the condemned man's screams. There can be no question that all this would deter far more killers than the quick, painless gas chamber. And we of the Committee foresee vast potentials in deterring other evils. If killing is bad, so is stealing. And so, unarguably, is double-parking. Several well-televised executions by the Chinese Water-torture Method for jaywalkers, for example, and our crime rate would unquestionably drop overnight. Not to mention our traffic problems.

The only possible opposition will come from a few bleeding hearts (the Christians, for instance) who will emotionally contend that torture is bad. And the Government shouldn't torture people.

Nonsense. Killing is bad. Yet we approve of our Government killing people in order to make an example for the rest of us. And, under this theory, it stands to reason our Government could make a far better example by torturing people to death. And we do so want our Government to set a good example. Don't we?

He Has Us in His Power

Who is the most powerful man in the world? President Johnson? Mao Tse-tung? General de Gaulle? Premier Nguyen Cao Whatshisname? Actually, as insiders know, he is none of these. The most powerful man in the world —the man whose every whim is instantly obeyed by millions upon millions of slavelike followers in a dozen nations —is, of course, Baron Homer T. Pettibone, head of that vast and secret international conspiracy known as SHEEK. In a rare interview transcribed in his castle deep in the fastness of Transylvania, the Baron incautiously revealed the barest of hints as to how his nefarious organization operated.

"White eye-bones! Heh, heh, heh," chortled the Baron, rubbing his hands in fiendish glee. "Command them all to paint their eye-bones white."

A hooded assistant scurried out the door with the order. White eye-bones?

"For years," explained the Baron, "I've made millions of

women paint their eyelids blue and green. Now I add a master touch—chalk white over the bone."

But why?

"What good is power if you don't exercise it? Watch this." The Baron snapped his fingers. "Up skirts another inch."

"Yes, Baron." An aide saluted and barked into an intercom: "Up skirts to four inches above the knee."

"Ha-hah!" cackled the Baron. "A million women will now uncomplainingly take another tuck in their hems. Up-down, up-down. Out-bosoms, in-bosoms. Up-waists, down-waists. Sleek hips, no hips. Sophisticated look, young look. Red lips, pale lips. Keep 'em hopping, I say, on their crippled feet."

Crippled feet?

"Ho-ho. First, I cripple them with pointy toes and spike heels. Now I assuage them with the rounded toe and chunky heel. What masochists I have in my grasp! Have them pin a horse's tail on the back of their heads."

A horse's tail?

"Hee-hee. We'll call it a 'fall.' Very SHEEK. And we won't tan them dark brown this summer. Make them all biscuit-colored. With weird pictures on their knees. 'Knack-knees,' ha-ha. Shall we paint their noses purple? Hmmm, wait till next year. In the autumn, I will deliver my crushing blow. I'll lower their skirts precisely one inch more than the hems they've tucked up. Oh, how ingenious. They'll need all new wardrobes."

Good Lord! That will bankrupt a million innocent husbands.

"Exactly!" cried the Baron, an insane gleam in his eye. "No one escapes the power of SHEEK."

Well, a few may doubt that millions of women have fallen into the clutches of an international conspiracy run by a madman. But is there a more rational explanation for the behavior of our ladies?

And I, for one, say the time has come for all free men to join in busting this vast, insidious plot. Before it busts us.

Put It On, Put It On

It was in 8104 B.C. in the prehistoric kingdom of Erotocea that mankind stumbled on a discovery which many historians rank with fire and the wheel in its wide-reaching effects on human civilization. The innovation was, of course, the topped female dancer. The discovery, as is often the case in the history of science, was accidental. A tavern owner, whose name has come down to us only as "Samm," was half-heartedly auditioning Erotocean maidens, seeking new entertainment for his jaded customers. A young lady painted purple and orange had just finished going through her gyrations with three pet gila monsters and a live eel.

"So what else is new?" said Samm with a yawn. "Next."

It was at this dramatic moment in prehistory that onto the stage stepped Miss Karul Dodo. She was never noted for either her beauty or her grace. But what distinguished her from all other maidens of the time, who of course went about bare from the waist up, was the fact that she was wearing a muu or tightly knit Erotocean sweater.

"Excuse it," she said apologetically. "I gotta bad chest cold."

"So, okay," said Samm with a shrug. "Dance."

Her performance proved slightly less than a terpsichorean masterpiece. Indeed, several times she tripped over her own feet. But as Samm watched, a strange light came into his eye.

"You've got something, kid," he said. "You're hired."

"Gee, thanks," said Miss Dodo. "And wait'll you see me perform without my muu."

"You ever do, kid," said Samm, "and you're fired."

The rest is prehistory. Crowds of the curious flocked to Samm's tavern to ogle this famed topped dancer. The ladies sniffed. "What's she got to hide?" they'd say. But the effect on the men was overwhelming. For the discovery unleashed one of the most powerful forces the world has ever known —the male imagination. In his mind, each man saw, under Miss Dodo's muu, the female form divine—the one he had always been searching for. And as she never shattered illusions by removing her muu, she consequently drove strong men mad with frustration and desire. Needless to say, the custom spread. The topped dancer was followed by the topped waitress and the topped all-girl band. Soon ladies of even the best families were wearing muus in public and, inevitably, muu-muus. Legions of Decency were formed under the slogan, "Take It Off!" Priests thundered from the pulpit: "If the Lord God Ur had wanted women to hide

their bodies, he would have created them with muus on."
But there was no stemming the tide. The birth rate soared.

"We must appeal to women to once again display their
charms openly," said a wise philosopher hopefully. "Or else
mankind will enter a period of decadence, immorality and
a snickering preoccupation with sex that could last ten thousand years."

It did.

Mickey Saves the World

Herewith is another unpublished chapter in that unpublished textbook *A History of the World, 1950–1999*. The
title of this chapter is "Today Disneyland, Tomorrow Disney World."

It was late in 1965 that Mr. Walt Disney, who created
Mickey Mouse out of an old bottle of ink, announced plans
to build a $100 million Disney World in the State of
Florida. This revelation filled the hearts of all Floridians with
joy. And they swore to call a special session of their Legislature, build a network of new highways and otherwise pre-
pare for Mr. Disney's coming. The instant success of
Disney World naturally led to the proposal that he take over
West Virginia. His triumph in creating a neat, clean Poverty-
land out of the abandoned coal mines and slag heaps is
well known. Tourists came by the thousands to ride the little
mine cars and throw pork chops and grits in hygienic, Saran-
wrapped packages to the well-scrubbed poor. Following that

success, the conversion of Washington, D.C., into History-land caused little notice.

And in 1973, when an electronically operated Congressman rose before a crowd of applauding tourists in the galleries to propose changing the name of the nation to "The United States of Disney Country," the measure passed unanimously. Actually, the Disneyans, as citizens were now called, lived much the same lives as before. They spent their days riding around in cars and their evenings being entertained by various machines, such as one that simulated live people moving about on a screen and another that simulated live music on a magnetic tape. The Disneyans still thrilled to the exploration of space. But they did so in simulated rockets. And they still plunged into the exotic watery depths, but in simulated submarines in artificial concrete pools. All of which was much safer.

The Nation was open from 10 A.M. to 10 P.M. every day of the year, and the annual festivals to Mickey and Minnie Mouse and the Great Dog Pluto attracted pilgrims from all over the world. The war in Vietnam ended in its fifty-third year with the conversion of that country to Jungleland. (The ride through the Mekong Delta with stuffed Vietcong firing blanks from the riverbanks proved the greatest attraction.) And with the establishment of Disneygrad the following year, it was only a matter of time before the entire world became a wholly owned subsidiary of Disney Enterprises, Inc. And what a utopia it was—neat, clean, orderly, with enough simulated thrills and artificial adventure for one and all.

Well, almost all. There was one old man (no one else

ever grew old) who missed the past. "I miss tears," he said, "and automobile horns and the smell of manure and the common cold and dandelions and getting drunk and how you feel when someone dies."

Naturally, he was declared insane and locked up in a windowless dungeon. But it was a neat, clean, well-lighted dungeon with a big television screen and twenty-four-hour Muzak. All Disneyans were surprised when he killed himself.

"After all," they said, "he had everything a man could want."

Part Two

THEY, THE LEADERS

The Old Campaign Trail

The Mother Figure

Senator Margaret Chase Smith has firmly announced her
intention of being elected our nation's first lady President
come November. And everybody's saying, "Ha, ha" or
"chuckle, chuckle." "Ho, ho," they say. "A lady President!
Just imagine her being awakened in the middle of the night
to make a grave decision. And she'd have to brush her hair
and put on lipstick. Because it's a well-known fact no lady
can make a decision without brushing her hair and putting
on lipstick. And by that time we'd be in the soup. Who'd
vote for her? Ha, ha."

Ha, ha, yourself. I say Mrs. Smith's a shoo-in. And I
say it with a shudder. For the election of a lady President,
gentlemen, means the demise of our democratic way of life.
Look at the record. Who, I ask you, was the only Republican
to make the White House in the past thirty years? Mr.

Eisenhower. And why did the public love him so? Because, as any psychologist will tell you, he was a father figure. And having a father figure in the White House to take care of us made us feel secure. The father figure became the ultimate weapon in American politics. And there's no question G.O.P. strategists will now turn to Mrs. Smith. For what she represents is the ultimate refinement of the ultimate weapon. She is (*shudder*) a mother figure. Oh, I can see her campaign now. First, her aides let slip that her secret nickname is "Ma." Next she gains forty pounds, dons gold-rimmed specs and an apron and goes around the country dusting flour off her hands and calling everybody "Son." Just looking at her will make you feel warm and protected. She'll carry every precinct in the nation, including Johnson City.

Well, you'll say, a father figure in the White House wasn't so bad. True. Like any father, Mr. Eisenhower would give us a stern moral lecture once in a while. But otherwise he left us pretty much alone. Mainly because he was out on the golf course trying, like any father, to get away from us kids. And no harm done. But a mother figure! The very essence of motherhood is totalitarianism. A good mother, gentlemen, is a benevolent despot. Oh, there's no question what lies ahead. The first Executive Order will be one of those simple pronouncements: "Everybody clean their plates." This will be followed by a tough Galoshes Law requiring the wearing of rubber overshoes whenever the sun isn't shining. A national curfew will be imposed to insure we get plenty of sleep. When our motherly President is cold we'll all have to put on our sweaters. And any back talk will be met with the supreme penalty: She will turn off the television.

Well, I realize it's the trend. I know we seem to demand more and more that our leaders love us, coddle us and tell us what to do. And perhaps our democracy can survive a paternalistic federal government. But a maternalistic one? Never!

Our only hope is that the Republican Party will see the peril, eschew an easy victory with Ma Smith and nominate one of its many male hopefuls, like Mr. Rockefeller, who is, at worst, a stepfather figure. For the essence of democracy is to keep electing leaders we don't really trust.

Boy American

Hi there, boys and girls out there in front of your TV set. Comfy? Well, hold on to your hats 'cause here we go—off on a brand-new thrilling adventure series with a brand-new thrilling adventure hero . . . GARY BOLDWATER, BOY AMERICAN!

(*Theme*: "The Stars and Stripes Forever.")

Faster than the speed of sound, stronger than the Chase National Bank, able to bound over tall issues in a single leap . . . GARY BOLDWATER, BOY AMERICAN!

Who will save us from the Communists? Who will save us from the Keynesians? Who will save us from ourselves? GARY BOLDWATER, BOY AMERICAN!

So c'mon, kids, let's join Gary today for "The Thrilling

Adventure of the Phony Treaty." There he is in his disguise as a stuffy old senator with his stuffy old horn-rimmed glasses and stuffy old double-breasted suit. That's his pretty secretary, Lotus Lane (who doesn't know who he really is either), handing him a document.

Lotus: Here's a copy of that nuclear test ban treaty, Senator Boldwater. Shall I read it to you?
Gary (who always pretends he can't read): Well, now, Miss Lane, I don't see much sense in that. The way I hear, it's just another simple old treaty. Nothing to get het up about.
Lotus (vexed): But, Senator. Look, it's written in two languages!
Gary: Now, now, Miss Lane. Heaps of things are written in two languages. Like . . . Well, like heaps of things.
Lotus (angrily): Oh, Senator, you're just like so many Americans. You're sweet, but you're so naive!
(She stomps out and Gary whips off his glasses and suit to reveal the uniform of a general in the U. S. Air Force Reserve! The uniform of . . . GARY BOLDWATER, BOY AMERICAN! Leaping into the cockpit of his very own jet plane, he zooms into the sky and circles over the Washington Monument.) Gary (musing as he flies in circles): There! Now I am able to think more clearly with my 100 I.Q. brain. Could Lotus be correct? Wait! I shall scan this document with my 20–20 vision. "The governments of . . ." Hmmm. ". . . discontinuance of all test explosions . . ." Hmmmmmmm. "In witness whereof the undersigned

. . ." Leaping lizards! Lotus was right! Our nation is in peril! Oh, that I shall but be in time to save the day!

(We shift to the Capitol, where our beaming Senators are about to ratify the treaty. Suddenly, through the skylight, crashes a parachutist. Could it be? Yes, it is! GARY BOLDWATER, BOY AMERICAN!)

Gary: Gentlemen, before voting you should know that one of the signatures on this pact is that of an "Andrei Gromyko," who is a proven card-carrying member of the Communist Party!

(There are shocked cries of "Oh, no!" and "Egad, sir, he's right!" The treaty is torn up. The Senators give Gary a Big Six before he can modestly slip away. Later, once again in disguise, Gary greets a breathless Lotus Lane in his office.)

Lotus *(glowingly)*: Oh, Senator, I wish you'd been there to see him. If only you could be more like that.

Gary *(winking at the camera)*: Well, Lotus, I guess we can't all be GARY BOLDWATER, BOY AMERICAN! *(turning serious)* But it sure would be a great country if we could.

Goodby, Mr. Eisenhower

"My name's Eisenhower," he said with a grin as he stepped up to the podium. "Dwight D., that is."

The reporters laughed appreciatively. They had stood when he entered the crowded conference room at the Hilton

Hotel. And now they began asking their questions, respectfully prefacing each with his honorary title: "Mr. President . . ." Yet each question was designed to draw him into the bitter battle that swirled through the city that lay outside. Was he still neutral? What about the platform battles over civil rights, nuclear weapons, extremism, prayers in the schools? Did he agree with Scranton on the threat posed by the Birchers? Where did he differ with Goldwater on foreign policy? Whose side was he on? Each time he would pause and then deliver a gentle little lecture. He spoke of our moral duties, the wrongness of extremism, the importance of religion. He told the reporters how foreign policy was made. And as he talked, I thought of my grandfather.

My grandfather was a good and kindly man, slender, silver-haired, dignified and respectable, eminently respectable. I was a boy and we lived in a big house on Oakwood Avenue in Dayton. Calvin Coolidge was President and we used to have lemonade on the side porch on Sundays after church. Each evening my grandfather would listen to Amos 'n' Andy on the radio. We had a Negro maid who was "one of the family." She was good to us. We were kind to her. We all knew our place. On Saturdays, the neighbor boy and I would play war. I had a tin helmet and I can still remember how the strap felt under my chin and the glory there was in being a soldier.

I remember how my grandfather took me fishing and how it was to sit on the bank of an Ohio creek, the bob floating in the water, and how the shade trees looked. And how the Fourth of July was then, how warm summer dust feels between your toes, and exactly how the bell on the screen door of the soda-fountain store tinkled. And I remember how my grandfather would tell me what my duties were about my obligations to my fellow men. Now, looking back, how clear and easy these seemed, how secure we were, in that pleasanter, nicer, simpler society of so long ago. Yet, I remember, I would shuffle my feet as he talked and wish he would hurry through so I could get outside and play. And I'm sorry for it now, because I loved him.

The reporters sat, doodling with their pencils and thinking of the next provoking question, as Mr. Eisenhower spoke of the importance of "common courtesy and good manners" and hard work and helping the poor. At last it was over. They stood respectfully as he left. Then they hurried excitedly out into the corridors to catch up on the latest bitter fight over the latest bitter issue. One paused and, nodding to where Mr. Eisenhower had stood, asked with a wry smile: "Do you think I can describe him as a party leader?"

And I felt very sad. For it never seemed more clear that the pleasant, nice, respectable party of Mr. Eisenhower's is gone. And so is my grandfather. And so is his world.

Give Us a Jingle

The historic 1964 campaign for the Presidency of the United States, on which the fate of mankind hinges, is now officially under way. Both Madison Avenue ad agencies involved have fired their opening 30-second TV salvos. As you undoubtedly know, the contenders this year are

Doyle Dane Bernbach, Inc., which is building a candidate called "L.B.J.," and Erwin Wasey, Ruthrauff & Ryan, Inc., which is promoting a product named "Goldwater." Between them, the two are expected to spend more than $10 million selling the public—almost one third the ad budget of the leading soda-pop manufacturer and as much as many makers of chewing gum. Which just shows how important the American Presidency is becoming.

Naturally, in keeping with modern advertising techniques, neither firm is saying anything good about its product or anything bad about its competitor's. Not directly. No, thanks to motivational research, subliminal perception and consumer-psychology studies, brutally frank statements are scrupulously avoided. And the message is put across by innuendo. Which, I feel, needs explaining. Take one of the dramatic, hard-hitting TV spots of Doyle Dane Bernbach's campaign for L.B.J. A telephone is ringing. A man's hand picks up the receiver. The announcer asks you: "Who [sic] do you want answering the phone when Khrushchev calls?"

Now, clearly, you will hope it isn't one of the children. You know how they louse up messages: "Some man called, Daddy, and was he ever mad about something and you better call him back right away only the dog ate up his number." So this is a strong pitch for L.B.J. Because he's a grownup and has a better chance of getting the message straight.

Erwin Wasey, Ruthrauff & Ryan, Inc., are striking back hard for Goldwater with the theme slogan of their campaign: "In your heart, you know he's right." At first glance, this tends to raise some questions. Such as: "How far right?" Moreover, it would seem to imply that in your head you know he's wrong. But actually, surveys show that most consumers think with their hearts anyway, except a small percentage who think with their stomachs. Additionally, motivational research proves the slogan has great appeal to the White blacklash, Negro frontlash and Oriental sidelash. Further, it brings up the whole subject of hearts. And L.B.J.'s is certainly suspect. Medically speaking.

Even from this brief summary you can see we're in for an all-out, thought-provoking campaign. For, personally, I find nothing more thought-provoking than modern advertising techniques. Every ad provokes you into thinking. And there's nothing more provoking than that.

Of course, with the fate of man hanging in the balance, I do worry that $10 million isn't enough. For as long as the Presidency's decided these days by the number of billboards, spots and jingles we consumers are bombarded with, I say this nation's in grave danger. Yes sir, it's in grave danger of being led for the next four years by a bottle of soda pop.

Good G.O.P. Breeding

Everybody's worried these days about the survival of our two-party system. You can hardly pick up a learned political journal without stumbling across an article entitled, "Whither the G.O.P.?" Which is just what it seems to be doing. Naturally, every expert has a theory to explain the growing preponderance of Democrats on our national scene.

These include reaction to Goldwater extremists, urban sprawl, the high-tariff policies of Mr. William Howard Taft and elm blight.

But if you ask me, the only expert who's seen right through to the heart of the problem is Mrs. Clare Boothe Luce, the eminent Republican and staunch Goldwater supporter. The reason Republicans are becoming more and more outnumbered, she gloomily told an audience of her fellow party members, is "because we are being greatly outbred by the Democrats." Mrs. Luce is absolutely right. A moment's thought will confirm it. Due to numerous factors, Democrats inevitably tend to multiply far more swiftly than Republicans. First of all, Democrats are poorer and thus tend to purchase more double beds. Being poorer, they also have less money to budget for outside entertainment such as *bal masques* and the like and therefore have more idle time on their hands in the evenings. Moreover, studies show Republicans have migrated to the suburbs in droves. So that a Republican gentleman, after a long and tiring day at the office, must fight his way through an hour's heavy traffic before he is in the arms of his loved one, and it's a wonder there are any Republicans left at all.

But these are merely contributory factors. Essentially the problem, let us face it, is breeding. And while generalizations are dangerous, I think it is sage to say that Republicans, on the whole, are more well-bred than Democrats. And being well-bred, of course, they don't breed as well. This trend becomes clear at an early age. Compare a typical young Republican lady and a typical young Democratic girl. The typical young Republican lady, as we know, wishes to be properly introduced, dances at arm's length, chats about music, art and Bryn Mawr fashions and engages in a soul-searching debate on the propriety of a goodnight kiss after the third date. As for Democratic girls, they are, undeniably, more democratic.

So Mrs. Luce is absolutely right. Now then, what are we who believe in the two-party system going to do about it? Because of the gravity of the problem, I'm sure, some will call for massive Government technical assistance, including subsidies and vast retraining programs. But I say that's not the Republican way. Nor can more private measures, such as more private Young Republican cocktail parties, alone meet the need. No, in our hour of crisis we must turn to that quality which made this country great—individual initiative.

And now if you'll excuse me, I've got to go put on my black tie, cuff links and pomade. Our American way of life is at stake, baby.

The Longer the Better

The frost is on the pumpkin. The long and grueling campaigns are all but ended. It is election eve. And at this decisive moment in history, it is the duty of us ace newsmen to assess the mood of the American voter. I've done dutifully so. And the mood of the American voter, gentlemen, is: "Thank God the whole thing's over." Indeed, in the past week 73,462,978 people have, publicly or privately, called for a change in our system of political campaigning. Of these, 73,000,000, would like to see shorter campaigns based on the British system, 462,971 would prefer cleaner campaigns based on the unlikely system, and 7 are urging no campaigns at all, based on the Russian system.

The exception is Mr. Gilbert S. K. Fanchot, who is demanding lengthier presidential election campaigns. Mr. Fanchot is chairman of the American Committee for a Do-Nothing Government.

In an exclusive interview Mr. Fanchot explained his unique position.

Q—Mr. Fanchot, you believe in longer political campaigns?

A—Yes. On the morning following a presidential election, under the utopian plan we've drawn up, the defeated party will immediately nominate its candidate for the next election. He will then promptly launch a long and grueling campaign.

Q—And the President would be forced to do likewise?

A—Yes. Ideally, I would like to see the new President and his new opponent each embark on a four-year whistle-stop tour of the country. In order to get their messages across to the voters.

Q—But certainly, sir, you realize that during a political campaign our Government is severely handicapped in its dealings with a crisis-ridden world?

A—Exactly. You will note that during this past campaign our Government was confronted with seventeen crises: the crisis of the Chinese atomic bomb, the crisis of the overthrow of Premier Khrushchev, and fifteen crises in South Vietnam. In each case it did the same thing.

Q—Nothing?

A—Nothing. In each case, the President, for fear of alarming the voters, postponed any decisive action until after the election. And in each case the result was the same.

Q—What was that?

A—Disaster was averted. Domestically, we thrived. For it is a widely held axiom that politicians can do nothing in an election year. And consequently, nothing was done to us. Indeed, the whole thing once again proved the immortal words of Benjamin Franklin: "He governs best who goes off on a whistle-stop tour somewhere."

Q—It certainly sounds as though you've drawn up an utopian plan to assure international peace and domestic tranquillity. But one thing, sir. Do you think the average American voter could survive a four-year campaign?

A—Well, back to the old drawing board.

The Power of Negative Voting

To the polls, ye sons of freedom! Stand up for your inalienable rights! Get out there and vote against the candidate of your choice. Excuse my exuberance this morning, but I always get all worked up on election day. It's the majestic climax of our whole democratic process. In the sacrosanct privacy of the voting booth, safeguarded from all retribution, masters of our destiny, we get to vent our spleen.

"Take that, you shifty-eyed no-good!" we cry, stamping our X opposite the name of the villain's opponent. "This is for you, you, you rascally wastrel!" we mutter, pulling the lever under the other fellow's card.

At last, our venom exhausted, we compose our features into a Jekyll-like mask of righteousness and emerge through the green curtains with a pleasant little smile for our neighbors waiting eagerly in line—fit and ready to face the tribulations of life once more. Oh, there is nothing finer for the soul! And, as elections go, this of course is a vintage year. What a fine crop of candidates to vote against. Even the most casual survey shows that hardly anyone will vote for hardly anyone—excluding, of course, the candidates themselves and their relatives. And I have my doubts about many of the latter.

It is widely believed, for instance, that Right Wing extremists will vote for Mr. Goldwater. Nonsense! They will happily cast their ballots against Fidel Castro, Walter Jenkins, Bobby Baker and topless bathing attire. There has also been some loose talk that Left Wing extremists are supporting Mr. Johnson. Balderdash! The Left Wing, as always, will vote with relish to crush creeping fascism, the military-industrial conspiracy and the Right Wing in general. Southern Democrats will march bravely to the polls to vote against uppity Nigras and all federal interference in the Southern way of life. Except for crop subsidies and the like. Negroes, in turn, will get their revenge for the past year's humiliations by voting vigorously against whatever smacks of White supremacy.

In contemplating this glorious blood bath, my sympathy

goes out to the moderates of both parties. They simply lack the deep-down vituperation required to get the most out of this day of days. You know how they feel: "Well, frankly, I don't care much for Goldwater, but I just can't stomach that Johnson." Or vice versa. And while they, too, will be voting against the candidate of their choice, I fear they won't put their hearts in it. Really, they don't know what they're missing.

But tomorrow is another day. Tomorrow, our souls cleansed of wrath, we will unite as one nation to bind our wounds and march forward shoulder to shoulder beneath the banner of the leader we mistrust the least. And that's fine with me. I think negative voting's the keystone of our democracy. Yes sir, if the day ever comes when we, the people, start having faith and trust in our leaders, then totalitarianism's just around the corner.

So allow me to join with the League of Women Voters, the Boy Scouts and other worthy organizations in urging you to get out and vote. For mental health, for democracy, for our American way of life, get out there and vent your spleen.

Heaps O' Horse Sense

Presenting Elbie Jay

We executives here at Another Network, Inc., have been checking over our television programs for the coming year. And we're in trouble. As you may recall, we have a heart-throbbing daytime serial going called *The Rocky Road to Happiness*, starring Rocky Nelson and his young bride Hysterical O'Brien. And for the kiddies, there's this jim-dandy adventure series—*Gary Boldwater, Boy American!* But what have we got to appeal to the whole family during prime viewing time? Nothing. So we've been working on it in typical creative tee-vee fashion. First of all, we asked ourselves: What are the two most popular programs on the air today? Well, *The Beverly Hillbillies* is No. 1, and *Bonanza* is a close second. Next, in typical creative tee-vee fashion we asked ourselves: What can we steal from both of them? And I think we've got the perfect combination. It's about the rooting-tooting, folksy Jay family who strike it rich. Only they aren't hillbillies. They're cowboys. And the pa of the family is Elbie. Yes sir, old Elbie Jay.

Elbie's kind of a cross between Walter Brennan and John Wayne. Lots of earthy horse sense but steely-eyed. And he's not known as "the fastest handshake west of the Pecos" for nothing. For he's the top wrangler in the whole of Texas, which, as you know, is the home of plain and fancy wrangling. Now Elbie's married to this pretty gal name of Birdie Bird. And they've got two cute teen-agers names of Myna Bird and Bye-bye Birdie. Plus plenty of lovable kinfolk like Aunt Jessie and Uncle Huffman and Cousin Oriole. And they all live down Texas way on "The Little Spread," where Elbie does a lot of hard work. Which is all for the Birds.

Then one day while mending fences he hits a gusher of Texas oil money. The whole family a-saddles up and a-heads back East to live in this big white house. Which they call "The Expensive Spread." And the Jays have many a rib-tickling adventure in high-class society, each one proving that folks are pretty much folks the worl' o'er, no matter which fork they eat with. And that when it comes down to problems, good old-fashioned horse sense sure does beat all. Meanwhile, Elbie's got his work cut out for him as foreman of The Expensive Spread. And it takes all his know-how as a top Texas wrangler to ride herd over these sharp Eastern galoots. But simple, homespun virtue always triumphs. Besides, any man who can wrangle his way to the top in Texas can hold his own in a wrangle anywhere. Moreover, in each action-packed adventure Elbie can always count on his faithful sidekick Sancho Pierre. Who also serves as sort of a foil for the hero's rapier-like horse sense.

So we've got a rollicking, thrilling plot, a cast of warmly human characters and a hero everybody can identify with. And all that's been holding up production is the lack of a title. We rejected *The Bonanza Hillbillies* as too familiar. While *The Wrangler* and *Birdsmoke* made it seem just another Western. But at last we're ready to roll. Yes sir, we have a title we feel captures the very essence of our new series, one which describes in a folksy phrase what every program will be full of:

Heaps o' Horse Sense.

Elbie Meets the Press

Howdy there, folks. How's things with you-all tonight? Welcome to *Heaps o' Horse Sense*, the rib-tickling tee-vee adventures of that rootin'-tootin' Jay family—starring ol' Elbie Jay, the friendliest wrangler ever to wrangle his way out of Texas. As we join Elbie, his pretty wife Birdie Bird, and their two cute tads, Myna Bird and Bye-bye Birdie, they've struck it rich and they've a-moved into this big white house back East. That's Elbie there now, a-pokin' through the East Room with his faithful sidekick Sancho Pierre.

Elbie: Right fine place. Soon's I get my initials branded on these fixings it's going to seem just like home.

Sancho Pierre (worriedly): Chief, the newspapermen are demanding a press conference and you've got to build your public image. Only you know them. They'll try to skin you alive.

Elbie: Well now, Pierre, any friends of yours are friends of mine. The varmints. You tell 'em we'll have one of them there ol' press conferences right now.

Sancho Pierre: Okay, Chief. I'll set up the State Department Auditorium. Let's see, Kleig lights, coaxial cables, Nielsen surveys . . .

Elbie: No sense a-goin' to all that fuss. Just you open that there door and herd 'em in.

Sancho Pierre (horrified): In here! But, Chief, that's unheard of. You can't build a public image in here.

Elbie: As my granddaddy used to say, "A mule down a gopher hole is worth six crows in the schoolmarm's tool shed." Just you leave it to me.

(Sancho Pierre hesitantly opens the door. One hundred and sixty-two slick Eastern newsmen rush in, eager for blood.)

Elbie (cool as a mushmelon): Howdy there, boys. Glad you-all could come chat a spell. Have a souvenir ballpoint pen and a souvenir ashtray. Had a little trouble getting my picture on them pens. Lucky I'm tall and lean.

Ace Newsman: Sir, what are your plans for increased monosodium glutamate exports to the Common Market in view of EFTA's opposition to the GATT agreements on . . .

Elbie: That's a right fine question you asked there, son. (Pierre, unscrew a souvenir doorknob for that lad.) And I want you-all to know we're a-working on that problem mighty hard. Now, boys, have you-all seen around this place? This here's my office and that there's the Blue Room. Skeedaddle along now. And this here's Birdie Bird's bedroom . . .

Birdie Bird: Elbie! You've just got to learn to knock.

Elbie: Now don't get your feathers ruffled, Birdie Bird. Our dear friends here have seen ladies in pincurlers before. And this here's our Myna Bird's bath. Oops, excuse us, Myna Bird. And this here's the back yard and that there's my horse on which I'm about to ride off into the sunset while you boys go write your mighty fine stories about my warm, lovable family and how I'm working hard on any problems you got on your minds. (And, Pierre, cut down a nice souvenir chandelier for each of the boys on their way out.)

Is this any way to build a public image? Do you think for a moment these smart Eastern newsmen will be influenced by folksy charm and personal attention? As usual?

So come and visit with us again, friends. And meanwhile, as you mosey on down life's long trail, remember: All it takes to build a public image is a heap o' horse sense.

The Dog Lover

Howdy there, folks. How y'all? It's time for another rip-snortin' tee-vee visit with the rootin'-tootin' Jay Family, starring ol' Elbie Jay, a very kindly cowpuncher. For a man who punches cows. As we join with Elbie tonight, he's in a heap o' trouble. That's him, a-gettin' ready to go on a tee-vee program in that big white house back East. And those fellers, a-pacin' back and forth, are what's called "party leaders." My, they look worried.

Elbie: I still don't see why I got to go on this here special tee-vee program. All I did was pose for the photographers, a-picking up my little old puppy dog.

First Leader (groaning): By the ears!

Second Leader (moaning): That picture will cost us the election. We've still got 97.2 percent of labor, business, the Negroes, the Southerners, the farmers and the consumers. But we've lost the dog lovers. And as the dog lovers go, so goes the nation.

Third Leader (bemoaning): Our only hope is this special television appeal.

Elbie: But I explained at the time why I pick up my puppy dogs that way. It's because, I said, I like to hear them yelp.

Leaders (together): Yelp!

Elbie (admiringly): You fellows have got that down right good. Isn't it a pretty sound? Reminds me of down home.

First Leader (groaning): Please, we never pick up a dog by the ears here in the East. Why didn't you raise rabbits instead? Or beat your wife? Or something we could explain. Well, there's nothing for it. Just go on camera with your fine family there and tell an alarmed nation how kindly you are. Ready, Birdie Bird? And Myna Bird? And Bye-bye Birdie? And Checkers?

Elbie: Checkers? That dog's name's not Checkers.

Second Leader: It is now. We wanted some nostalgia on this show. Okay, roll 'em.

Elbie (sincerely into the camera): Evening, folks. Mind if I mosey into your living rooms a spell? Because I want to tell you tonight how kindly I am. "Kindlier than a hound's tooth," they call me.

First Leader (whispering from off camera): Good, good!

Elbie (encouraged): Yes sir, folks. Notice how my wife Birdie Bird's not wearing any of those furs which require killing little animals. No sir, she's wearing a good S.P.C.A. cloth coat. And my little puppy dog's ears aren't an inch longer than when we left home.

Second Leader (whispering): Great, great! Now, pick up the dog fondly. But remember, not by the ears!

Elbie (nodding): No sir, friends, I always lift up dogs the way the kindly Eastern folks do. See? (*As he holds the dog up for display it lets out ear-splitting squeals and kicks over cameras and lights.*)

Third Leader (emerging from wreckage sadly): Well, wait till '68. But tell me one thing: why did you pick up that dog by the tail?

Elbie (puzzled): Now, friend, how many handles you think a dog's got? (*With a smile of sheer delight.*) But wasn't that the prettiest sound you ever did hear?

Well, folks, that's all for tonight. Except for this bipartisan message to dog lovers and Elbie lovers alike: Chip in now for our fund to buy ol' Elbie a brand-new dog. Yep, friends, for his own good we're going to surprise him. With a Great Dane.

Elbie Meets His Equal

Howdy there, folks. How y'all? Time for another tee-vee
visit with the rootin'-tootin' Jay Family, starring ol' Elbie
Jay—a humble fellow who believes in never lordin' it over
his equals. If'n he should ever meet one. As we join up
with ol' Elbie today, he's a-settin' at his writin' desk, pen in
hand, scratchin' his head and lookin' angry. That's his faithful sidekick, Robin (Texas Jack) Valenti, at his side.

Elbie: You know, I just can't figure that varmint out. I give
him nothing but kindness. I treat him like an equal. I even
mentioned his name once or twice in my public statements.
And then he wants to go his own independent way.
Robin: Fulbright is an ungrateful rat.
Elbie: Him too. But I'm talking about the sneaky polecat
who really stabbed me in the back.
Robin: Old Ho is an ungrateful dirty rat.
Elbie: Him, too. But I mean old Chuck de Gaulle. Just
think of him, wantin' to get out of NATO. You know what
it all boils down to, Robin? He don't trust me.
Robin (shocked): No!
Elbie (nodding): Yep, It's hard to believe. After all, what's
life without mutual trust? The sneaky polecat. But what am
I going to say about a fellow like that in this here speech I'm
writin'?
Robin: Well, here's a line I just read, sir: "No nation
today can hope to pursue an isolated course. Without the

full consultation, approval and material aid of her allies, she is bound to be defeated."

Elbie (*happily*): A decent, kindly, aboveboard statement, Robin, and a credit to my sense of fair play. Where'd you get it?

Robin: I think it's what he said about your war in Vietnam.

Elbie (*pounding his hand on the table*): See what a sneaky polecat he is? How can you trust a fellow who'd say a thing like that? Worst of all, how can I outfox this varmint, if I can't figure out what makes him tick? What do I know about him?

Robin (*reading from a file*): Well, he's a big, tall man. Very vain about his personal appearance and photographs. Awfully petty about protocol. Hardly ever holds press conferences because he doesn't like to be questioned.

Elbie (*ticking them off*): Vain, petty, clever . . .

Robin: Plays off one faction against another domestically. Says what the voters want to hear. But his basic drive is to go down in history as the most wonderful leader his country ever had.

Elbie: Devious, demagogic, overweeningly ambitious . . . (*grudgingly*) He must work mighty hard.

Robin (*nodding*): It's like he had extra glands. But to sum up, sir, he thinks he's the greatest man in the world.

Elbie (*snapping his fingers*): That's it, Robin! You've found the key. But, great balls o' fire, how are we going to deal with a fellow who thinks he's me?

Robin (*blanching*): You're right, sir. Oh, I'll sleep each night a little worse just knowing a man like that is their President.

Well, tune in to our next episode, folks. And meantime, as you mosey on down the long trail of life, remember what Elbie's ol' granddaddy used to say: "There ain't nothin' more precious in life than trust. So get all you can."

Elbie Is Appealing

Howdy there, folks. How y'all? Time for another tee-vee visit with the rootin'-tootin' Jay Family, starring ol' Elbie Jay—the most appealing cowpoke ever. He's always appealing. To everybody. To do something.

As we join up with ol' Elbie today, he's a-talkin' into the telephone as his kindly foreman, McGeorge (Smiles) McBrandy, bustles in, frownin' grimly.

Elbie (into the telephone): Now, Gen'ral, about that there situation in Vee-yet-nam . . . Hang on a minute there, Gen'ral. What's on your mind, McGeorge?

McGeorge: It's about that appeal you made to everyone, sir, to see America first this year.

Elbie (beaming): Yep, that was one of my finer appeals. First, I explained to folks about the dollar drain. Then I appealed to their high sense of duty not to go traipsin' off overseas tossin' money around. And I hit 'em a lick in their patriotism, sayin' a strong America requires them to stay home this summer. My, I get all choked up thinkin' about it.

McGeorge: Well, the first results are in, sir.

Elbie: I reckon the steamship companies are complainin' they're going broke?

McGeorge (nervously): Not exactly, sir. As a matter of fact the number of American tourists going abroad is smashing all records.

Elbie: Great balls o' fire! Now why do you think folks aren't doin' what I appeal to them to do? We got to stop the dollar outflow. We got to bring every American home. (*Into the telephone*) What? No, not you, Gen'ral. I want you to send another 30,000 troops to Vee-yet-nam.

McGeorge: But, sir, there must be 10,000 tourists on their way to London right now. And another 20,000 to Paris.

Elbie (shaking his head): And another 20,000 to Paris. (*Into the telephone*) No, no, Gen'ral, not another 20,000 to Paris. Chuck de Gaulee wouldn't cotton to that. Make it another 20,000 to the Dominican Republic instead.

McGeorge: And a small army of tourists will be descending on Moscow.

Elbie (irritably): And a small army to Moscow! (*Into the telephone*) No, Gen'ral. Not to Moscow. That'll take a big army. Well, I know. But there must be someplace we can send a small army. I'll put my mind to it.

McGeorge: Of course, sir, looking on the bright side, you're constantly gaining widespread support throughout the world. Indeed, in Latin America there are signs everywhere backing your stand.

Elbie (pleased): That so, McGeorge? What do they say?

McGeorge: "Yanqui, Stay Home!"

Elbie: McGeorge, you're a regular whiz! You've just solved the whole consarned problem.

Elbie (*happily into the telephone*): Gen'ral I changed my mind. Send 20,000 troops to Paris, 5000 Marines to the Riviera, a brigade or two to the Greek Isles, a couple of companies to Rio, a battalion and a half to . . .

McGeorge: But, sir, how will this help get our tourists to see America first?

Elbie (*cheerily*): The way we're going, McGeorge, there won't be another place that'll have 'em.

Will Elbie's campaign to keep Americans home by sending Americans abroad work? Tune in to our next episode, friends. And meanwhile, as you mosey on down the winding trail of life, remember what Elbie's ol' granddaddy used to say: "Always appeal to a man's better judgment. If'n nothin' else'll work."

Fastest Deal in the West

Howdy there, folks. How y'all? Time for another tee-vee visit with the rootin'-tootin' Jay Family—starring ol' Elbie Jay, who always deals from the top of the deck. If'n it's his deck. As we join up with ol' Elbie tonight, he and his pretty wife, Birdie-Bird, are just a-settin' down to a hand of bridge with the man he loves and trusts above all others, the man he elevated to the second highest office in the land, the unforgettable fighting moderate, Hubert Horatio Whatshisname. Making the fourth is Mrs. Whatshername.

Hubert (*holding Elbie's chair*): Well, well, and how are you feeling tonight sir?

Elbie: Always thinking of yourself. Don't forget that I gave you your job. I gave you fame and power. I made your name into a household word. And don't you forget it, Homer.

Hubert: It's Hubert, sir.

Elbie: There you go, always trying to get your name mentioned. And speaking of that, didn't I see your name in the paper this morning. That's twice in six months, Herbert.

Hubert (*blanching*): Honest, sir, it was an accident. A traffic accident. I ran over a little old lady, and a reporter with an encyclopedic memory recognized my name.

Elbie: Well, don't let it happen again. There's no room for publicity seekers around here. The papers only got so much space. Now, let's see. You shuffle there, Birdie-Bird. That's it. Shuffle them good. And you cut, Higbert. That's right, cut them a couple of times. And I'll deal. Hmmm. I reckon I'll take these thirteen cards here, and you folks can divvy up the rest, fair and square.

Hubert: Gee, that's a fine deal, sir. Would you like to bid now?

Elbie: Seven no-trump.

Hubert: Gosh, that's a brilliant bid, sir. And I haven't even seen your hand.

Mrs. Whatshername: I'm afraid I'll have to doub . . . Ouch!

Hubert: She passes too, sir.

Elbie: A fine woman. You may all be seated now. And I'll just lead this little ol' king of hearts here . . .

Hubert: A marvelous lead, sir. I'll just have to play my little old three of hearts . . . Whoops!

Elbie (thunderstruck): You played the ace!

Hubert (pale and trembling): Honest, sir, it was an accident. I strategically planned to eat the ace later when you weren't looking. I reached for the three, but my hands were all sweaty and . . .

Elbie: Another accident? Hmmm. I always said, Hirschel, that your eyes were set mighty close together.

Hubert (pleading): On, please don't say you don't trust me, sir. I'll kill myself.

Elbie: What! And get your name in the papers? You wouldn't dare.

Can Hubert find happiness in humble obscurity? If he knows what's good for him? Tune in to our next episode, folks. And meantime, as you mosey on down the trail of life, remember what Elbie's granddaddy used to say: "Happy is the humble man who don't expect a great deal. But he ain't near as happy as the dealer."

Elbie's Big Mistake

Howdy there, folks. How y'all? Time for another tee-vee visit with the rootin'-tootin' Jay Family, starring ol' Elbie Jay—an open-hearted feller always willin' to admit a mistake. No matter what Republican made it. As we join up with ol' Elbie today, he's holdin' one of his regularly scheduled tee-vee press conferences. Which he regularly schedules every couple of years or so. And, my, he sure has got a wily look in his eye.

Elbie: . . . And let me say again that I'd go anywhere and do anything in the cause of peace. Anything, mind you, anything.

Reporter: Then why, sir, did you escalate the war in Vietnam?

Elbie: I'm glad you asked that question, son. I want to take this opportunity to tell the whole world that (*He pauses, chokes, sputters and finally manages to speak in a barely audible whisper*) . . . I was wrong!

(*There is a moment of stunned silence. Then, as one man, the reporters rush for their telephones. Later, Elbie and his trusty top hand, Wild Bill Moyers, are analyzing the results.*)

Wild Bill: Congratulations on your historic first, sir. You captured banner headlines in all the dailies, and every national magazine is saluting you as the first leader in world history ever to admit he was wrong.

Elbie: Never mind the trimmings. What about the polls?

Will Bill: Just as you predicted, sir, the country's rallying behind you in this crisis. You're up 48 points.

Elbie (happily): Oh, it's good to have faith in the polls once again. And the stock market?

Wild Bill: It went 32 points down, 27 points up and 17 points sideways.

Elbie (frowning): I was hoping to shake it out of its normal pattern. How is the State Department taking it?

Wild Bill: With horror, sir. Your orders for them not to issue a clarification paper caused three undersecretaries to attempt suicide by leaping out windows. Fortunately, in keeping with the spirit of the Department, they all chose ground-floor windows.

Elbie: You can count on them. What about diplomatic circles?

Wild Bill: Absolute chaos, sir. Seventeen nations have withdrawn their ambassadors for instructions on how to deal with a country whose leader is not infallible. But they can't find any precedents. Meanwhile, seeing how well it's helped you at home, they're all trying to emulate you. De Gaulle claims he's been wrong three times.

Elbie: He's always bragging.

Wild Bill: And the Communists are really trying to outdo you. Kosygin's talking about bringing back Khrushchev, Mao Tse-tung's confessed he can't swim, and Ho Chi Minh wants to negotiate. It looks, sir, like peace in our time.

Elbie (grandly): Well, I said I'd do anything for peace, and I did it.

Wild Bill (admiringly): It must have taken a lot of courage, sir, to say in public that you were capable of human error.

Elbie (nodding): Yep. I never thought I'd get away with a whopper like that.

Well, tune in again, folks. And meantime, as you mosey down the trail of life, remember what Elbie's ol' Granddaddy used to say: "You can always profit on your own mistakes. But it's a sight easier on someone else's.

Elbie Plans a Family

Howdy there, folks. How y'all? Time for another tee-vee visit with the rootin'-tootin' Jay Family—starring ol' Elbie Jay, a proud daddy who wants his daughters to marry young men with bright futures. So he always fixes one up for them. As we join up with ol' Elbie today, he and his pretty wife, Birdie Bird, are a-settin' in the parlor as their oldest tad, Myna Bird, comes bouncin' in with a handsome young feller.

Myna Bird: Mother, Daddy, we're engaged!

Elbie: My, so your young man popped the question, honey? At last. I can't tell you what a happy surprise this is, and here's the guest list I worked up for your wedding. I thought you'd like to ask all the fine Congressmen whose votes I need and a couple of your friends, too.

Myna Bird: Please, Daddy . . .

Elbie: Then we got to think about the honeymoon. Ohio looks best to me.

Myna Bird: Ohio! Why, Ohio?

Elbie: It's a swing state. And after that it'll be time to start planning a family. I'm planning on you to start having it by November, '68. Late October'd be best, I reckon. I don't want to peak too early.

Myna Bird (angrily): You're not losing a daughter. You're gaining a couple of points in the opinion polls.

Elbie (happily): More like six or seven. (*Frowning*) But what am I going to do with you, young man? Now that boy

Pat Whatshisname, who married my other tad, Bye-Bye Birdie, he's proved himself a comer. (*Proudly*) Why, he's already a television-station executive, a bank director and a leading Texas citizen. (*Sadly*) My only regret is that I have but one television station to give to my family.

Young Man: Oh, don't worry about me, sir. I'm going to Vietnam next March.

Elbie (*surprised*): Going to Vietnam! Then how come you're marrying my daughter? Don't tell me you're getting too old to play romantic leads.

Myna Bird (*wringing her hands*): Daddy, he's not George Bulova, the actor.

Elbie (*peering over his glasses*): Why, so he isn't.

Young Man: I'm a captain in the Marine Corps, sir. That's why I'm going to Vietnam. I plan to make it my career.

Elbie (*delighted*): Why, that's wonderful news, Major. Just think how folks'll take to me having a member of my own family over there, Colonel. So when you get there, General, tell Westmoreland he's done a fine job and I'm sorry to replace him. Oh, I'm mighty pleased, son, you decided to make a career in my other family business. (*Suddenly scowling*) But what happened to that George Bulova fellow? I thought you were going to marry him.

Myna Bird (*near tears*): He never asked me.

Elbie: Never you mind, honey. I'll announce your engagement myself to him. That'll make that polecat sorry.

Myna Bird: I don't think he cares.

Elbie (*rubbing his hands*): He will when he gets my engagement announcement. Let's see: "To George Bulova. From Me. Greetings . . ."

Well, tune in to our next episode, folks. And meantime, as you mosey down the trail of life, remember what Elbie's ol'granddaddy used to say: "When a feller's given you a dirty deal, think big and don't try to get even with him. Try to get ahead."

Going Hollywood

The Smile of Ronald Goodheart

Once upon a time there was a young man named Ronald Goodheart who could smile well. His smile was warm, winsome, boyish, friendly, unassuming and utterly charming. In fact, it was the most winning smile in the whole wide world.

"Gosh," he said, smiling to himself in the mirror, "blessed as I am with a smile like that, I should go far."

And he did. He went to Hollywood, where he smiled in 132 movies. His smile was a tremendous box-office success. Even the critics found no fault with it. And across the land it melted middle-aged matrons by the millions.

"Gosh," said Ronald Goodheart, "blessed as I am with a smile like that, I should go further." So he went down to the public-relations firm of Batten, Botten, Button & Osgood and told them he wished to run for Governor. Mr. Batten laughed. Mr. Botten snorted. Mrs. Button choked.

And Mr. Osgood said: "What makes you think you could be elected Governor?"

Ronald Goodheart just smiled.

B.B.B.&O. immediately took the account. It was a grueling campaign. Ronald Goodheart took his smile from one end of the state to the other. He showed it to a thousand audiences, big and small. And every time he smiled he won another ten thousand votes. His panicky opponents said he used to be a Left Wing nut. Ronald Goodheart just smiled. Then they said he used to be a Right Wing nut. Ronald Goodheart just smiled. Finally they said he didn't know a single darned thing about being Governor. Ronald Goodheart just smiled. And he won in a landslide.

Of course, his smile was all Ronald Goodheart had. He could also, when Communism, dope or smut were mentioned, frown. And he could also, when civil rights, poverty or slums were mentioned, look sincere. But his smile was what counted. And no one was surprised when his party unanimously nominated it (and him, too) for the Presidency. Another grueling campaign followed. Ronald Goodheart took his smile on whistle stops from coast to coast. On election eve, the polls showed him ahead 98 to 2. And so he strode confidently into the studio for the Great Television Debate, munching on a pastrami-on-rye sandwich.

Just as the cameras began to roll, down came his upper jaw and a sesame seed lodged between his frontal incisors. A hidden flaw cracked, widened and split. And with a sickening crunch one tooth shattered! In this moment of adversity, in full view of a nationwide television audience, Ronald Goodheart responded to fate's cruel blow in the only way he knew how: He just smiled.

Needless to say, he lost the election 62,789,338 votes to 14. And today he is playing character parts on the Chautauqua circuit, mumbling in his cups about purchasing a bridge and launching a comeback. But the pros just shake their heads. You can't elect a man, they say, with an artificial smile.

Moral: In the complex arena of modern American politics you cannot struggle to the top on a smile alone. You got to have sound teeth.

Little Miss Candidate

Real Life Presents . . .

LITTLE MISS CANDIDATE

Starring
Ronald Reagan as The Governor

With
George Murphy as The Senator

And Introducing
Shirley Black

(*Open on cheering crowd. Close in on Shirley on platform taking bow after bow. Pan to Ronald and George waiting in wings, frowning. Shirley skips up, breathless.*)

Shirley: Golly whillikers, wasn't that wonderful? Real life's just like the movies.

Ronald (forcing a smile and squeezing her hand): You wowed 'em, honey.

George (squeezing her other hand): You sure made us proud, honey.

Shirley: Gosh, Mr. Murphy, you're not mad, then? Both of you seemed so dead set against me running.

George (patting her hand): We just didn't want to see a sweet kid like you mixed up in a racket like this.

Shirley: Gee, that's what you said to me in *Little Miss Muffin.* Real life *is* just like the movies. And just think, we'll all be together again in Washington—Mr. Murphy in the Senate, Mr. Reagan in the White House, and me . . .

Ronald (grimly): I guess it's time to tell you, honey. I'm afraid we won't be together in Washington.

Shirley (round-eyed): But everybody says I'm going to win.

Ronald: That's just it, honey. You see, honey, there's some mean folks in the world who think movie actors running for office are pretty funny. And when you get elected to Congress, it's going to make George and me look downright ridiculous.

George (dramatically): Don't worry, honey, I'm sure there's a job for an ex-hoofer like me somewhere. *(He tries a buck and wing and stumbles.)*

Ronald (dramatically): And who wants to live in the silly old White House anyway? Nancy says its no neighborhood to raise kids.

Shirley (her lower lip puckering): Golly sakes, what can I do?

Ronald and George together (eagerly): Withdraw?

Shirley (sticking out her chin): Like you told me in *Little Miss Lollipop*: "Never be a quitter, kid."

Ronald (with a grimace): I can't tell you how happy you're making us. And don't worry, honey, George and I will stand behind you.

Shirley (clapping her hands): Goodness, you mean you'll give me kindly, fatherly advice to help me win through, like in *Little Miss Sugar Plum*? Gee, real life is even more real than in the movies.

Ronald (happily): You're absolutely right, kid. Now first, you should come out for more pornography. That'll appeal to the sadomasochistic whiplash.

George (enthusiastically): Right! Then, after you've proposed a statue to Stokely Carmichael . . .

Little Miss Hawk

Real Life Presents . . .

LITTLE MISS HAWK

starring
Ronald Reagan as The Governor
George Murphy as The Senator

and Introducing
Shirley Black

(*Open on steaming jungle. Pan to three figures slogging through a swamp—Ronald, George and Shirley. Shirley's in the lead, a battered helmet on her curly head, an M-16 rifle over her shoulder. She's singing to keep spirits up.*)

Shirley: On the good ship . . .

George (*wearily collapsing on a fallen log*: It's no use, Shirley, I can't go on.

Shirley: Golly whillikers, Mr. Murphy, you've just got to!

Ronald (*dropping beside George*): You've got to remember, kid, that we're not as young as we were in *Little Miss Muffinchop, Little Miss Merrytwinkle,* and *Little Miss Mopeymoppet.*

Shirley: But, jiminy Christmas, Mr. Reagan, the whole Free World's counting on us to win through and give that awful Mr. Ho Chi Minh what's coming to him.

Ronald (*with a sigh*): What's the use? How can we buck a spineless administration committed to a no-win policy?

Shirley (*clasping her hands and looking heavenward*): Oh, please make Mr. Reagan our President. Then we can bomb the smithereens out of them.

Ronald (*automatically flashing a modest grin*): I am not a candidate. At this time. (*Glumly*) And sometimes I think I'll never be.

Shirley (*taking his big hand in hers*): Oh, please, Mr. Reagan, don't ever say that. Don't you remember what you told me in *Little Miss Morninglory?* "No matter how hopeless it seems, kid, you got to keep trying," you said. "I just know you can learn this new routine by opening night."

Ronald: That was George who said that.

George (his head in his hands): How can I go on and win this war, kid? I'm nothing but a broken-down old ex-hoofer.

Shirley (her lips puckering, her eyes filling with tears as she tugs at his sleeve): Oh, please, Mr. Murphy, don't ever say that. You're not a nobody. You'll show people. Don't you remember what you told me in *Little Miss Meadowlark?* "There's no people like show people, kid, when it comes to running the show."

George: That was Ronald who said that. In his last campaign.

Shirley (angrily stamping her foot): I don't care! There's all those folks out there in the Free World counting on you to go on, and you two sit there like bumps on a log *(thrusting forth her lower lip).* Well, I'll just have to go on by myself.

(She levels her M-16 and blazes away at the surrounding jungle, shouting through her tears, "Take that, you dirty Commie rats! And that and that and that!" The two men, shamed by her example, jump to their feet and begin firing, too.)

Ronald (proudly): I guess the kid's just about the greatest little Hawk in the world.

George (equally proudly): Who'd have thought she could ever play a role like this?

(Fade on chatter of automatic rifle fire, the whine of bullets and the screams of dying Commie rats. Musical theme, "Bless America," swells up and out.)

Sir Ronald of Holyrood

I.

The Budget Killer

All right, children, climb up on daddy's knee and he'll tell you another fairy tale about Sir Ronald of Holyrood. Let's see. How about Sir Ronald's awesome battle with the Budget? Ooo, it's scary! Try not to shriek in daddy's ear.

Well, as you remember, Sir Ronald had vanquished the Evil Governor, freed the Golden State, and banished the Wicked Wizard from the Castle of Cal. And so it was that he buckled on his famed Swinging Sword, mounted his white charger and set off on the most dangerous quest of all —to penetrate the Thorny Thicket in whose thorny depths dwelled the Unruh, feared by one and by all.

"I know you will follow, me, Sancho," said Sir Ronald confidently to his faithful squire Sancho Nofziger. "For you have purity, decency and righteousness in your heart."

"And," muttered Sancho with a sigh as he clambered aboard his donkey, "rocks in my head."

Hardly had the two companions rounded the first bend in the Thorny Thicket than a huge, indescribable shape loomed up in the gloom.

"Quick, sire, flee!" cried Sancho in alarm. "We are face to face with a Budget!"

"What, Sancho," said Sir Ronald, bravely standing his ground, "is a Budget?"

"Oh, sire," said Sancho, falling to his knees, "the Budget is a vast, incomprehensible thing that thrives in this turgid murk. Your predecessor, the Evil Governor, for who knows what diabolical purposes, fattened it up year after year so that it now threatens to topple over and crush the simple people of our beloved Golden State."

"Hola, Budget, yield!" cried Sir Ronald. "For to save my people from being squashed by your loathsome bulk I shall lop off a tenth of your flabby fat and trim you down to size."

But a strange thing happened. No sooner had Sir Ronald drawn his Swinging Sword than the air was filled with piteous cries and heart-rending groans.

"What manner of strange creature is this?" asked Sir Ronald as Sancho covered his ears and cowered. "I have not yet struck a blow, yet already we are knee deep in blood and tears. Do people love the Budget so?"

"Oh, no, sire," said Sancho, "all abhor it. But everyone loves some part of it. And each fears you will wound the one he loves."

"Courage, Sancho. To save our people we must strike boldly. Take that, you swinish Budget, and that and that!"

And Sir Ronald sliced and hacked and hacked and sliced and . . .

Now what are you crying for, children? The Budget? For goodness' sakes, don't worry about the Budget. It's a very magical beast. And the more Sir Ronald slices at it, the bigger it will grow. So that after the awful battle it will be bigger and fatter than ever. Honest.

What do you mean, you don't believe daddy? The trouble with you kids, damn it, is you don't have any faith in fairy tales.

II.

The Taxes Killer

All right, children, one more fairy tale about Sir Ronald of Holyrood. How about the time Sir Ronald met the Taxes? Well, get comfy and wait till daddy downs his martini. Let's see, when we last left Sir Ronald and his faithful squire Sancho Nofziger, they were hacking their way through the Thorny Thicket in search of that dread creature, the Unruh, who dwelt somewhere in its murky maze. Suddenly a huge and fruminous beast, all gobbly-jawed and prickly-spined reared upward in the gloom ahead.

"Have at you, varlet," cried Sir Ronald, drawing his famed Swinging Sword and shouting his battle cry, "For Purity! For Righteousness! For Just Plain Goodness." He fearlessly prepared to hurl himself on his foe.

"Hold, sire," said Sancho tugging at his master's doublet. "Spare yourself the energy. The awesome beast is the Taxes. And it is magically indestructible."

"What is the Taxes?" asked Sir Ronald.

"Oh, sire," said Sancho with a shudder, "It dwells here in the Thorny Thicket, growing ever larger. Then each spring, it emerges from this place and descends upon your beloved people of the Golden State, gobbling up their provender and inflicting great pain. It is why they hate the Thorny Thicket so."

"And rightly," said Sir Ronald, nodding solemnly, "for it is an evil, devious, incomprehensible labyrinth which all good people should despise."

Just then, from a converging path ahead a whole covey of little creatures bounded forward. They looked strangely like miniature versions of the Taxes, yet their spines were soft, their teeth barely formed and their whole appearance cuddly.

"What manner of wee beasties are these?" asked Sir Ronald, picking one up and examining it.

"Careful, sire," said Sancho with a worried frown. "Those are the Withholding Taxes. They would go out among your beloved people once a week, rather than once a year, nibbling, nibbling."

"Why they hardly hurt at all," said Sir Ronald, petting the one in his arms.

"Yes, sire," said Sancho sagely, "and for that reason I suspect they are a trap set by the Unruh to woo your beloved people away from their hatred of the Thorny Thicket."

"Oh, my poor people," cried Sir Ronald and with his Swinging Sword he quickly dispatched the Withholding Taxes, each and every one. "Ah, how my people will love me for this good deed," he said.

"For Taxes, Sancho, should hurt. And now throw that huge surviving creature some food. I have decided he should grow even larger."

"Grow?" said Sancho in surprise.

"Taxes that hurt are good for my people," said Sir Ronald nobly. "And, verily, I can hardly wait until next spring. For never will they have had it so good."

"Now that sounds logical," Sancho muttered to himself as he scratched his head. "I wonder why I keep getting this uneasy feeling that I'm following some kind of a nut?"

Now, now, children, don't cry. I'm sure the Taxes won't eat everybody up, no matter how big. Look, if you want to cry, come around next April 15 and daddy will cry with you.

III.

The Tantalizing Treasure

All right, children, climb into beddy-bye and Daddy will tell you just one more. Let's see, how about the story of Sir Ronald and the Tantalizing Treasure? Well, as you remember, Sir Ronald and his faithful squire, Sancho Nofziger, had barely entered the Thorny Thicket in search of the Unruh, that fearsome creature who dwelt somewhere within its murky depths. Sir Ronald had dismounted from his handsome white charger and with his famed Swinging Sword he was cutting a brave swath through the magical Bureaucratic Brambles, which screamed piteously at every nick, almost as though they were human.

"Hola!" said Sir Ronald suddenly, raising the tinted visor

that kept falling down over his eyes. "What manner of enchanted vision is this I decry far off to the east?"

"What does it look like, sire?" said Sancho, as usual glad of any excuse for a rest.

"Why," said Sir Ronald, drowning, "it would seem to be a big white house that somehow shimmers and glitters, advances and recedes, looms large and fades. A mirage, if I be not mistaken."

"Oh, no sire," said Sancho happily. "It is the Tantalizing Treasure! How fortunate we are. While all shining knights who pass this way see it, few have drawn this close. Look, it is now almost within your grasp!"

"Hmmm," said Sir Ronald. "Why should I grasp for it?"

"Why, sire," said Sancho surprised, "it is filled with fame and power and treasures beyond one's imagination. Quick, to horse! We must pursue it lest some other knight captures it first."

"Hold, there, varlet," said Sir Ronald irritably. "I have pledged my sacred word to serve the people of my beloved Golden State for four long years, here in the Thorny Thicket. And I am not about to skeedaddle off after some Tantalizing Treasure."

Sancho was amazed. "But, sire, the Tantalizing Treasure always casts an enchantment over any knight who sees it. Invariably, he flies off in all directions spouting oratory, slaying mythical dragons . . ."

"Oh, I felt the temptation," said Sir Ronald, nodding. "But I merely mumbled my battle cry, 'For Purity! For Righteousness! For Just Plain Goodness!' And I gave no further thought to yielding."

"But, sire, the fame, the fortune, the . . ."

"A pox on fame and fortune; I shall not seek the Treasure." Sir Ronald resumed hacking straight ahead, allowing only an occasional glance over his shoulder to the east. "Of course, you might keep an eye on it, Sancho," he added, "in case it comes seeking me."

"Verily, sometimes I think I serve the most clever of masters," said Sancho to himself proudly. Then he scowled and scratched his head. "Either that, or he is some kind of nut."

All right, children, sleepy-pie. No, you'll just have to wait and see how it all comes out. There, there, I know you can hardly wait. Daddy feels the same.

Political Wisdom from All Over

The State of Happiness

Mr. Ravenwing McFlower, the hippie candidate for Mayor of San Francisco, has announced "a positive, dynamic program aimed at improving the welfare of all citizens." Asked if he could sum up this forward-looking public-welfare program in a few well-chosen words, Mr. McFlower nodded gently and smiled his quiet smile.

"Yes," he said, "people shouldn't get up in the mornings."

Mr. McFlower, an unemployed tin-can player, was in a loquacious mood as he met the press on the wide expanse of well-manicured lawn in front of his home, a teepee in Golden Gate Park.

"Actually," he said, rhythmically clanking two tin cans together as he contemplated a marigold. "I've studied a number of federal, state and local public-welfare programs, and none seems a whit concerned with the basic thing they should be concerned about."

What was that?

"Why, making people happy," said Mr. McFlower in some surprise. "Gosh, if you're concerned about someone's welfare, the first thing you hope is he'll be happy. It's no wonder this country's full of unhappy people who lead unhappy lives day after day.

"So I started thinking about what's the first thing that makes people unhappy every day. It's getting up. Of course, some people like to get up early, and if that makes them happy they should. Sleep when you're sleepy, I say."

"People have to eat, too," said an older reporter, somewhat sarcastically.

"Yes, I've also been thinking about that," agreed Mr. McFlower. "And I think people ought to eat when they're hungry. Almost everybody eats when he isn't and I'm sure it's not good for you. It's like the drinking problem. If people only drank when they are thirsty, there wouldn't be any problem about drinking, would there?"

"Look here," said the older reporter irritably, "the Government can't go around telling people how to lead their lives."

"Excuse me," said Mr. McFlower apologetically, "but if people get mixed up in a public-welfare program, it does. The Government tells you that you can't spend more than $14.32 or something a week for food and you've got to live in a concrete housing project you don't like and take a dreary job you don't like and so on. It may be concerned with the public's welfare, but it sure doesn't give a fig for your happiness."

A young reporter asked Mr. McFlower how he would enforce his program.

"Great Krishna!" exclaimed Mr. McFlower. "I wouldn't force anybody to do anything. I'd love them instead."

Naturally, Mr. McFlower's sweeping public-welfare program came under immediate attack.

"It is not the function of government," one of his opponents sternly told a rally, "to make people happy."

The solid citizens in the audience nodded wisely to each other and applauded to show that whatever the issues of this campaign might be, they certainly knew this was true.

The Making of a Leader

Senator Thomas H. Kuchel, square-faced and deep-voiced, sat in a leather-cushioned alcove in the ornate lobby just off the Senate floor and talked of the crucial decision he had made—the decision not to run for Governor of California. It was no easy decision. As the Senator relived it, he sometimes frowned, sometimes ran his hand through his hair and sometimes, when he spoke of the Right Wing, he swore. He talked of duty and of security, of ambition and of happiness. Nor was it an unimportant decision. It will have a great effect on the politics of California and Washington. And maybe the Nation. It was a very important decision. Perhaps even a historic decision. And yet, as he talked, you had the odd feeling of having made many such decisions yourself.

He talked first of duty. Was it his duty to return to California in hopes of uniting his badly divided Republican Party behind him by running for Governor? He was by far the strongest candidate the moderates had. And yet, if he tried, could he do it? The polls showed movie actor Ronald Reagan well ahead in the Republican primary. The conservative and Right Wing contributors would be in Reagan's camp. Money would be tight for moderates. What if the other moderate candidates refused to withdraw? They would split the moderate vote. It looked like a long shot. And yet . . .

If he could get by Reagan, the polls showed he should be able to lick the Democratic incumbent, Governor Brown. And there he'd be, the new Governor of the biggest State in the Union, the state with the most electoral votes. A new Governor, a decent, honest man, not too liberal, not too conservative, and 1968 was coming up . . . Why, some of his friends practically had him in the White House already. Of course, frankly he didn't want to be President. Wouldn't have the job for a million dollars. Why anybody would want to be President was beyond him. And yet . . .

Two women constituents fluttered up to inquire about tickets to the Senate gallery. The Senator was on his feet, warm and gallant, sincerely enjoying himself as he pointed the way down the corridor to his office.

Then, too, what about his duty in the Senate? He was already minority whip, in line perhaps to be the next leader of his party on the floor. Here he was liked and respected. Here he debated the gravest issues facing mankind. Here he was happy. And here, you felt, he was secure. Had he made the right decision. He laughed. At least he was glad it was over. And yet . . .

He had to go back to the floor. He strode past the marble busts up the marble steps. The guards nodded respectfully. The walnut-carved doors were opened for him. He stepped onto the thick carpet. A colleague grabbed his arm and said something. They both laughed. And yet . . .

Outside in the wet heat, Pennsylvania Avenue stretched away a long mile to where the White House glistened in the sun. And suddenly I thought of a sailboat race I'd been in.

On the last lap, I'd seen a chance to drive my boat between an outcropping of rocks and the shore. I was behind. I hesitated and then took the long way around. I lost. Later, I told myself I'd done the right thing. After all, winning truly wasn't that important. And yet . . .

The Favorite Son

With President Johnson and Richard Nixon both slipping in the polls, the emergence of a fresh, new candidate was not unexpected. The revelation came in a nationwide poll asking voters the routine question: "If Lyndon Johnson and Richard Nixon are the nominees of their parties, which candidate would get your vote?"

In reply, 7.2 percent said Johnson, 6.8 percent said Nixon and 61.4 percent said Jesus Christ. The remainder was split among lesser-known candidates. The surprising showing of a candidate whose influence had so far been felt in American politics created a sensation. Support was strong in the Bible Belt. Doves were enthusiastic over what they believed would be The Candidate's position on Vietnam. And indeed, no political figure voiced anything but unqualified approval in public. Both major parties vied with each other in saying how much they had long admired The Candidate and espoused The Candidate's principles. Spokesmen for each expressed confidence The Candidate would accept a draft to head their ticket. Initially, then, the Nation looked forward to a landslide. But a few cracks began to appear in this consensus.

The Candidate's known view on money-lending caused shudders on Wall Street and the Dow-Jones average plummeted 30 points. In general, the Eastern Establishment was cool, murmuring discreet remarks about "working-class background" and "radical social view." Hate literature, such as *The Cross and the Flag*, published exposés of The Candidate's ethnic background, causing more than one expert to worry in print, "Is the Country Ready for a Jewish President?" Negro militants denounced the doctrine of "turn the other cheek" as "just another Honky trap." And Conservatives, while praising The Candidate's record of feeding the multitudes, noted that this tended to sap individual initiative and the multitudes ought to feed themselves. Liberals talked uneasily about "separation of church and state" and the churches, as usual, couldn't agree on anything:

As quickly as the boom had soared, just as quickly did it fizzle out. Overnight the issue was dead. Everyone agreed that The Candidate, while praiseworthy and all that, simply wasn't electable. Many expert reasons were given, but a hard-headed politician, who had carefully studied The Candidate's record and voter appeal, went to the heart of the matter.

"Basically, it was the image," he said. "Beard, robes, a lot of talk about love—how would it come across on TV? People aren't ready for stuff like that.

"These days," he said, shaking his head, "a candidate like that would get crucified."

The Girl in the Lobby

Young ladies of the evening seem much in the news. One was busy overthrowing the British Empire. Others are practicing human brotherhood at the U.N. On a fee basis. And now various state capitals have been rocked by the scandalous news that nefarious lobbyists are employing young ladies to influence our legislators. Which is certainly scandalous. If not news. Where, I ask you, will it all end?

If you're not worried yet, let me tell you what happened at last night's session of the Greater Southwest Centerville Sanitary Control District Board, which I was attending as an interested citizen. I was about to enter the august Board Chambers (a sixth-grade classroom during daylight), when I was approached by a once-young lady in a black velveteen evening gown, false eyelashes and a feather boa.

"Honey," she whispered in a husky voice as she stroked my cheek and looked deep into my eyes, "buy Katzenbacher's Cast Iron Sewer Pipe. I go with it."

Thank you, I said, but I didn't happen to need any sewer pipe at the moment. I was just a simple interested citizen.

"Pardon," she said, squinting at me. "My eyes aren't what they used to be. I thought you were Board Member Alvin Battersbee. He's the swing vote on the new contract."

Was she herself, I asked delicately, perhaps a young lady of the evening in the pay of nefarious sewer-pipe lobbyists? "Young!" she cried happily. "Honey, I will tell you the story of my life for free." And she did:

"My name," she began, "is Mehitabel Pinkham and I have not always been in the low circumstances you find me now. Once I was the rage of six continents, attending only the largest international conferences representing naught but the finest cartels. *Toujours gai, toujours gai.* Ah, how well I remember Versailles. (That Clemenceau was a real tiger, honey.) And the London Naval Conference. (Those British sailors!) And when you read of how the League of Nations collapsed of sheer exhaustion, I can only say modestly that I was there. *Toujours gai, toujours gai.*

"But now the times had passed me by and I am reduced to representing Katzenbacher's Cast Iron Sewer Pipe. And, honey, *toujours gai* Mr. Katzenbacher ain't."

I thanked Miss Mehitabel and said that in view of the furor caused by the current scandals it was surprising to hear her type had been active in politics for years. "Honey," she said with pride, "lobbying is the oldest profession. And I personally have swung more issues than the League of Women Voters combined."

No offense, I said, but was it moral? "Moral!" she replied with an indignant flick of her ivory cigarette holder. "Nobody objects when a lobbyist gives a lawmaker a free lunch, a free theater ticket or a free campaign contribution. Why such a fuss when he's given a free me?"

Well, I'm sure none of us would agree with Miss Mehitabel's clearly immoral analogy. And I know you'll be happy to hear the nefarious Mr. Katzenbacher didn't get the sewerpipe contract. It went instead to a Mr. Graftendorfer, who presented Board Member Battersbee with a free case of whiskey, which, as you know, is perfectly acceptable these days.

Which all goes to prove that under our code of public morality, virtue will triumph in the end. Either that, or Miss Mehitabel is growing old.

Rags to Riches

Once upon a time, there was a poor little boy who lived in a poor little town. His family was poor. His friends were poor. He was very, very poor. His name was Horatio Alger. Although he was poor, young Horatio was filled with the ambition and fortitude which has made our nation great. "I will press on through life," he said, squaring his little jaw, "and become a rich man." At first, he determined to go to Wall Street to begin his career as a humble shoeshine boy whom some tycoon would befriend. "But no," he said, "it would be wiser to go to the place which has the most money in the whole wide world." So he went to Washington.

Horatio was fourteen years old when he came to Washington to make his fortune. He began as a humble Senate page boy. His duties were lowly and the pay a mere pittance. But his heart was filled with resolve.

"It matters not that I am poor and uneducated," said little Horatio, clenching his tiny fists. "For America is the land of opportunity. I shall work hard and I shall study hard. And I shall listen to the Senators I serve, for they are the wisest and most successful men in our nation. And thus I shall make my fortune."

So while the other little pages idled away their spare time in carousing and loose living, our Horatio worked hard, studied hard and sat at the feet of the Senators to learn the secret of success. He observed how friendly and generous they were, even with wealthy businessmen. He observed how happy they were to do favors for others. And how happy others were to do favors for them. And he marveled at how, despite such generosity, all grew richer. "Truly," he said, "the secret to success is to be friendly and generous." And he was. He did little favors for the Senators, pluckily rescuing their little bills when in danger of being run over by some committee. And in no time, the Senator from Texas, who was the cleverest man in the Senate, made him his personal assistant. And the Senator from Oklahoma, who was the richest man in the Senate, looked upon him as a son. And they taught him all they knew.

But success did not spoil Horatio. He forged ahead, doing bigger and bigger favors for all. In reward for such virtue, businessmen offered him profitable investments, bankers begged to lend him money, and the Senators were proud to call him their friend. Thus he grew up admired, respected and worth $2 million—a shining example to little boys everywhere that all it takes to struggle up the long path from rags to riches is hard work, generosity and pluck.

Ah, that our story could end here. But, alas, our Horatio fell upon evil times. Jealous rivals accused him of the worst crime known to Washington: "Influence peddling"—or doing favors in hopes of reward. Friends and fortune fled him. None was more shocked than the businessmen and Senators who had guided him all through his youth and young manhood. They called for hearings and probes and investigations. "How," they asked each other, sadly shaking their heads, "Could a fine young man like that have gone wrong?"

Moral: All it takes today to struggle up the long path from rags to riches is hard work, generosity and pluck. But don't forget to cover your tracks.

The Riddle of the Middle

The New Right has a shining new hero in Mr. Ronald Reagan. The New Left has a bold new action group called The National Conference for New Politics. To meet these threats it was inevitable that a new group should coalesce called "The New Middle." Typical of The New Middle is Mr. John B. Middlerode, a middle-aged, middle-height, middle-weight member of the middle class from the Middle West.

Q—Mr. Middlerode, could you tell us who comprises The New Middle?

A—Well, yes, I guess it's mostly members of the Old

Middle who have moved over. In this fast-changing day and age you can't just keep doing the same old thing.

Q—What primarily does The New Middle do that distinguishes it from the Old Middle?

A—We worry more. You see, we felt we were in danger of losing members from the Middle who might slip over the edge to the New Right or New Left. So we analyzed the function of the Middle and found it consisted primarily of worrying. Thus we conceived of our militant new action program of worrying more.

Q—Most constructive. And what do you worry about?

A—Oh, you know, the stock market, who's going to win the pennant, aphis, time payments, funny noises in the transmission, lung cancer, crab grass and thinning hair. The usual.

Q—Is that what all the members of The New Middle worry about?

A—Oh, no. The Ladies' Auxiliary worries about children's grades, what to have for dinner, drip-dry shirts, gray hair, what to do on Sunday afternoons, and getting worry wrinkles. Of course, that's only a very small portion of the many, many things The New Middle worries about.

Q—What about politics?

A—Politics?

Q—Yes, are the members of The New Middle Democrats or Republicans?

A—Invariably.

Q—But don't you worry about political goals?

A—Sure, I guess so. I mean lower taxes and government efficiency and things like that.

Q—What about specific issues? Do you take a position, for instance, on Vietnam?

A—Oh, yes, usually at cocktail parties. We agree that it's an awful mess and we ought to end it as soon as possible.

Q—How?

A—Well, you know, one way or another.

Q—Do you picket or march or . . .

A—Good heavens, we're not radicals! Oh, we may write an occasional letter to the editor decrying the lack of a stop sign at a school intersection. You know, some worthwhile cause.

Q—Would it be fair to say, then, Mr. Middlerode, that The New Middle really doesn't care about politics?

A—Yes, I guess that's true. But the reason we don't care much is that we know this country is in very good hands and has been for years.

Q—Whose hands?

A—Why, ours, of course.

The Economy? As Long As It's Healthy

In Its Usual State

In case you missed Mr. Johnson's State of the Union Address, you are probably sitting there right now, gnawing your nails and worrying: "What *is* the state of our Union?" Well, fortunately, I happen to have just such an address handy myself. Indeed, it's called The Handy All-purpose State of the Union Address. It's good for any President in any year. And, best of all, it doesn't matter a whit what kind of state the Union's in. The text follows.

Fellow Americans, I'm proud to report to you that that glorious nation is in glorious shape. Never seen it looking better. Fit as a fiddle. But credit where credit is due, friends. It's all due to your wisdom and foresight. In electing me President.

Yes, sir, I needn't tell you the sorry shape this glorious

nation was in when the Other Party was in office. Why, it was just about to gasp its last gasp. But despite their constant carping and heel-dragging, I'm proud to say I've somehow managed to lift up this bedraggled nation single-handedly and make it glorious once again.

So today, friends, thanks to my miraculous efforts, you never had it so good. I've got a bushel basket of statistics here which show conclusively we've now got the richest, mightiest, soundest, most glorious nation in the whole wide world. And we don't have a thing to worry about, friends. Except that this nation's in terrible shape. Frankly, folks, I've never seen it look so poorly. It's got unemployment, poverty, illiteracy, riots, blight (elm and urban) high taxes, farm surpluses, polluted water and falling hair. To tell the truth, I'll be mighty surprised if it lasts the night. And while I'm at it, I might as well inform you the state of the world isn't much better. True, my firm, astute foreign policy has insured a just and lasting peace forever and ever. But, confidentially, the whole shebang could blow up any second.

Now I hope I haven't alarmed you by my objective diagnosis of the state of the Union. Even though it does lie at death's door, friends, there's no cause for panic. Because, by a fortunate coincidence, I just happen to have a sure cure for every single one of the invariably fatal ailments it's plagued with. Naturally, I don't wish to bore you right now with the details of how I am going to save our sorry, bedraggled, sickly nation. But rest assured, I'll let our Congressmen in on my little secrets at the proper time. And I'll bet they'll be glad to administer my guaranteed remedies. Now that we all know what an awful state we're in. Once they've done that, friends, you can be sure our nation will be in glorious shape again—as glorious as it was up there in the first paragraph of my speech. . . . Thank you and goodnight.

So that's the state of our Union: gloriously healthy as it lies on its deathbed. And oddly enough, research shows that, according to our Presidents, it's been in that same schizophrenic state for at least the past hundred years.

Well, personally, nothing renews my faith that we shall long endure more than these annual State of the Union addresses by our Presidents. After all, if we can endure them, I say, we can endure anything.

The Big-time Spenders

Welcome, Ladies. Welcome to the 1984 Convention of our Society for Patriotic Consumption. And now let us place our hands over our hearts and recite: "A penny saved is un-American."

Fine. As this is our twentieth anniversary, I thought it might be best to open with a brief review of the tremendous strides our patriotic group has made in only two short decades. It was back in 1964, may I remind you, that the first great breakthrough occurred in our nation's economic thinking. That was the year in which a farsighted Con-

gress passed the first piece of major legislation designed to
do away forever with such outmoded vices as thrift, economy
and saving for a rainy day. I am speaking, of course, of
the revered $14 billion tax cut of 1964. The thinking be-
hind it was unassailable: by giving people more money to
spend, the more they would buy. The more they bought,
the more our factories would hum and the richer our nation would grow. How obvious! And thus, ladies, it was in
1964 that spending won its rightful place as the first duty
of every patriotic citizen.

Initially, this great economic truth was not realized by
all. And it is to the early heroines of our Society we pay
tribute tonight, those who devoted their lives to setting good
examples: Mrs. P. Craswell Knight, who spent $1162.18
at a sale of chenille bath mats; Mrs. Copley Tugglesworth,
who dragged home two bird cages on a peak-hour bus during the delivery strike; Mrs. Liz Burton, who . . . But, ah,
the names are legion. And the abuse good women suffered!
"Compulsive spenders," they were called. "Acquisitive
buyers." And even "neurotics." Can you imagine an era
which confused pure patriotism with a neurosis?

But by 1970, thanks to their efforts, thrift had become
a misdemeanor in seventeen states, and saving money a felony. Who among us can ever forget the banner day when
the Supreme Court upheld the conviction of H. Alger for
hoarding $2.32 in a cookie jar? Each subsequent year
brought its successes. Technological advances kept apace:
new miracle fabrics that ripped on unwrapping; water-sol-
uble umbrellas; disposable kitchens; and new wonder drugs
which caused fabulously expensive reactions. Shoddy crafts-

manship spread, creating demands, as did wonderful new slogans such as: "Seven cars in every garage, two TV sets in every bathroom and a psychiatrist on every couch." And as for our Congressmen, they at last proved themselves true leaders of the people. For who can deny that our current defense budget of $6.3 trillion sets a new high in patriotic squandering? But we cannot rest on our laurels. Let each of us, weary though we may be, get out there and buy, buy, buy: spend, spend, spend. Let us each selflessly do our utmost to preserve our new American way of life.

Nor let us forget that even today there are still those who cling stubbornly to the old ways. Let us in the years ahead persevere in our unending struggle to convert this one last sector of the economy to the virtues of spending. Yes, ladies, impossible as it may sometimes seem, let's all go home and keep trying to convince our husbands.

Government Doesn't Pay

Herewith is another chapter in that standard unpublished reference work *A History of the World, 1950–1999.* The title of this unwritten chapter is "The Rise of Private Government."

The trend toward private government was first noted in California early in 1967. In a bold move to cut rising government costs, Governor Ronald Reagan instituted the new concept of seeking voluntary donations to the State from its citizens. His early triumphs included the gift of a new

Governor's Mansion from wealthy contributors, a free efficiency survey of state agencies by 150 high-level private executives, and two days' work on holidays from state employees. This concept was quickly seized upon in Michigan by Governor George Romney, who asked all citizens to give four hours a week to civil programs that might otherwise be paid for out of rising federal taxes.

As virtually all citizens were against both high taxes and big governments, the concept snowballed. Special fund-raising events were organized for various agencies. The annual Mother's March for the Pentagon was always a huge success. And it was generally agreed that the Combined Salvation Army and University of California Bands playing on street corners at Christmas time were all that kept both institutions going. The voluntary donations of time to the state were another matter. But in 1973, Miss Oriole Hotchkiss, a staple remover in the Bureau of Pedicare, was the first civil servant to give 365 unpaid twelve-hour days to the state. She became a national heroine overnight. Others flocked to emulate her example.

Helping immeasurably, of course, was the Young Republican Guard, or "Right Guard," as it became known. These cadres of dedicated youth patrolled the streets, and woe betide the tired middle-aged man who, on being asked for a weekend's work for the Government, replied weakly, "But I gave at the office." As more and more citizens proudly volunteered more and more time to the state, problems developed. Private industry was being depleted of workers, and the volunteers, being unpaid, had to go on welfare. But all this was solved by the state assigning volunteers to essential private jobs and establishing state-run soup kitchens, manned of course, by volunteers. Taxes had dropped to a mere pittance, and all that remained was to do away with such costly, non-profit-making institutions as Congress, the Judiciary and the Presidency. The President, as was fitting, was replaced by a voluntary Chairman of the Board—the first being Mr. Jeremiah M. Mowe.

"Fellow volunteers," he said proudly in his inaugural address, "we have today established the first private, non-tax-supported government in the history of the world—a totally free government."

"High taxes and public spending," he said, "were leading us inevitably down the path to communism. But by abolishing both forever we have unquestionably saved ourselves from that dread evil."

And, oh, how the serried ranks of volunteers that stretched before him cheered.

"Huzzah!" they cried. "Long live Chairman Mowe!"

Taxes Make You Guilty

Heigh-ho, it's coming up income-tax time. And I think it's surprising how many people these days don't want to pay all the taxes they owe. I mean as a matter of principle. Take my pacifist friend Mr. Ira Sandperl. He says 60 percent of our taxes go for armaments to kill people with. He deeply believes killing people is immoral. So, as a protest, he's only going to pay 40 percent of his taxes. Of which, unfortunately, 60 percent will go for armaments to kill people with. Or the Negroes. Why, asks Mr. Dick Gregory, should he contribute to federal aid for Mississippi's White Supremacist government? And why, demands the White Supremacist in turn, should he be made to pay for the Civil Rights Commission? The Right Wingers are rightly outraged at having to give their money to Mr. Tito. While the Left Wingers are leftly outraged at having to give their money to Mr. Franco. It seems everybody's mad at some Government project they help support. The only solution to this growing trend is, of course, Selective Taxation.

Under this plan, you simply attach a little note to your tax return specifying how you want your money spent. Like: "Dear Government, here's the $384.23 I owe you. Please send it to the Chad Republic, as it's got a nice ring to it."

Right away, you can see how good Selective Taxation will make you feel. Would more thermonuclear bombs increase your sense of security? Buy a couple for your Strategic Air Command. Are you fond of Mr. J. Edgar Hoover? Make one big give for the FBI. Perhaps you've long been an ardent admirer of the Rural Electrification Administration or the Federal Oleomargarine Advisory Board? Well, here's your chance to show your appreciation. Naturally, each Government agency will have to compete for our tax dollars, justifying directly to us skeptical taxpayers its staff, its budget and the good it claims it does. And we will enjoy direct democracy at last.

Of course, I suppose we will have to put up with some splashy promotion campaigns by the larger departments.

Such as: "The Pentagon Needs Your Help!" And I assume the smaller agencies will be hard hit. Indeed, I foresee droves of seedy-looking characters with shoddy attaché cases ringing our doorbells to make their pitches for the Diaper Research Commission Fund or some such. But that's just pin money. Besides, I plan to unscrew the bulb in my porch light. Anyway, such minor inconveniences are a small price to pay. For there we'll be, a nation of happy taxpayers, all of us warmed by the thought we are giving to causes we believe in, our consciences clear. No longer will we be forced to pay for actions we deem immoral, to be responsible for what we feel are the misdeeds of our Government. No longer . . .

Hold it! Good heavens, Selective Taxation is unworkable. I mean most other agencies may stay in business, but who's going to give to the Internal Revenue Service? Voluntarily?

Well, back to the old Form 1040. And a guilty conscience.

Wall Street Is Watching You

Once upon a time there was a funny-looking beast called a Stock Market. It had the head of a bull and the tail of a bear. Or maybe it was the other way around. Because nobody could ever tell which way it was going. Sometimes it went up, which made everybody rich and happy. And sometimes it went down, which made everybody poor and sad. As it affected their lives so directly, the people naturally had a deep and mystic faith in the Stock Market. They worshiped the incantations of its priests, who would chant things like "making a temporary readjustment" when the market went down, and "reflecting a healthy economy" when the market went up. Then, one day, the market reflected a healthy economy by making a temporary readjustment. Zooommm-SPLAT!

Panic and bewilderment ensued. Nobody could explain why the market had decided to go down rather than up. Nobody, that is, except the noted market analyst Dr. Homer T. Pettibone.

"The Stock Market," he explained, "is not only a wondrous-looking beast, it is endowed with extrasensory perception. It knows what we're thinking. And it is eager to please us. Therefore, it moves whichever way we think it will move. If most of us think it will go up, it goes up. And if most of us think it will go down, it goes down. If we think it's a bull, it's a bull. If we think it's a bear, it's a bear. This is the sole factor that controls its movement. Thus all we need do to be rich and happy is to think rich and happy thoughts."

And it worked! Everybody agreed to think the Stock Market was going to go up. So, thinking it would go up, they gave it offerings of money. Consequently, it went up and up and up and up. And everybody grew rich and happy. No one was prouder than Dr. Pettibone. He showed his young son, Homer II, his thousands and thousands of receipts for the offerings he'd given the market. "One day, son," he said, beaming, "these will be yours."

"I'd rather have an apple," said Homer II.

"But these are certificates of our faith in the Stock Market, which is half bear, half bull and endowed with extrasensory perception. It's what makes you rich and happy."

"There's no such animal," said Homer II. "It's a mythical beast."

At first, Dr. Pettibone was shocked. Then he was thoughtful. Then he picked up the phone and whispered: "Sell short."

When the news leaked that Dr. Pettibone himself had lost faith in his theory, everybody thought the market would go down. And with everybody thinking that . . . Well, zoommmmm-SPLAT!

"See," said poor Dr. Pettibone sadly to his poor, sad son as they stood in the bread line, "I was right all along."

Moral: The things you've got to believe in to be rich and happy these days you wouldn't believe.

Blue Chips Go to War

Herewith is another unpublished chapter from that invaluable reference work *A History of the World, 1950–1999.* This chapter is entitled, "How the Free Enterprise System Was Saved."

It was in the summer of 1966 that the United States realized something would have to be done about the stock market. For generations, stock-market fluctuations had controlled the economy. If stocks went up, the nation prospered. If stocks went down, the result was depression, unemployment and widespread poverty. Yet, oddly enough, while there were a thousand esoteric theories, no one really knew what made stocks go up and down. Sometimes people would pay more for them, sometimes they wouldn't.

"The economic strength of our country is far too important to leave to the whims of private investors," said the President. "Even if they are all widows and orphans."

"The insoluble problem," said a noted economist, shaking his head, "is that more people want to sell stocks at the moment than want to buy. We therefore have a surplus of stocks."

"A surplus, eh?" said the President, perking up. "Well, let us handle that in the American way."

And thus, in an historic move, jurisdiction over the stock market was given to the Department of Agriculture. The Secretary of Agriculture, in the American way, immediately devised guaranteed floor prices for all stocks based on 90 percent of parity. When any stock dropped below its floor, the Government promptly purchased enough shares to drive the price back up again. Soon, silos and granaries from one end of the country to the other were bulging with Government-owned surplus stock certificates. In an effort to slow down the accumulation of these surpluses, quotas and certificate-printing allotments were imposed on all major brokerage firms. A few shady promoters, however, managed to make killings under the Stock Bank Plan by not issuing new stocks they had never planned to issue anyway.

But the most far-reaching change came when Congress, in an effort to reduce surpluses, included stock certificates in the Surplus Commodities Program. One can only imagine the joy of the destitute in Appalachia on opening their weekly package to find not merely the usual pound of lard, sack of chick peas and can of powdered milk, but ten shares of General Motors. The poor, no longer poor, purchased new clothes to attend the stockholder meetings. The investors, having as much confidence in the market as in the Government itself, bought, bought, bought. And stocks soared to undreamed of highs.

Due to the immutable economic theory that when stocks go up, prosperity results, the whole world grew fabulously wealthy. There were two cars in every Asian garage and a chicken in every African pot. It was the ultimate victory of capitalism and the defeat, of course, of world Communism.

For, as Mao Tse-tung himself said with a sigh on ordering another thousand shares of Titan Missiles, Inc., from his broker: "Better rich than Red."

Oh, For the Bad Old Days!

Rising prices, soaring interest rates, the critical lack of unemployed workers . . . Has no one the answer to the manifold headaches we face in an inflationary, affluent society? Yes! Fortunately, a little band of militant do-gooders has been formed to strike directly at the heart of our current economic problems. They call themselves "The League To Bring Back the Depression."

"Two chickens in every garage!" cried the League's Executive Director, Mr. Homer T. Pettibone, at a mammoth rally. "Business may be booming temporarily, but let us have faith that a depression is just around the corner."

The crowd, composed of well-dressed persons of middle age or more, sighed nostalgically. "Ah, those were the days!" said one.

"Right!" said Mr. Pettibone. "I remember I first went to work making ninety-eight cents for a sixteen-hour day."

"Hah!" shouted a heckler triumphantly, "I got seventy-two cents and three pig's knuckles for a seventy-hour week."

"There you are," said Mr. Pettibone. "There is a ground-swell in the grass roots to bring back the Great Depression. None of us who lived through that great experience can help but recall with fond memories and pride the pittances we received. And the more affluent we are today, the more we yearn for those lost years.

"I ask you corporation executives out there, are you plagued with exorbitant union demands, high labor costs, a shortage of qualified workers?"

"I remember," said an elderly gentleman with a sigh, "when we'd hang up a 'help wanted' sign and a hundred men would line up, hats in hand."

"Right!" cried Mr. Pettibone. "And you matrons, have you got servant problems?"

"Oh, those days when you could get a nice, polite couple for fifty dollars a month and keep," said a buxom lady with a sigh. "And not uppity, either."

"Right!" cried Mr. Pettibone. "And you housewives, how are prices?"

"I recall when milk was eight cents a quart," said a

slender lady with a sigh. "And you could get a seven-course dinner for fifty cents. With wine."

"Right!" cried Mr. Pettibone. "High prices, high taxes, high living. Our kids grow up soft and spoiled with every convenience. We never had it so good and it's awful. Let's bring back that *esprit de corps* we once enjoyed. Let's bring back those simpler times with simpler pleasures. Let us, my friends, put our shoulders to the wheel, our noses to the grindstone and Bring Back the Depression!"

The crowd went mad. Carried away by Mr. Pettibone's ringing words, they voted unanimously, as a first step, to cut his salary to fifty cents an hour. Since then, enthusiasm has spread like wildfire.

Unfortunately, however, the work of the League has been temporarily brought to a halt while a replacement is being sought for Mr. Pettibone as Executive Director.

We'll Tax Your Mind

"I see where the President has figured out a new tax," said the Kindly Old Philosopher admiringly. "You'd think folks would applaud such a feat of ingenuity."

What new tax?

"The way it come about," said the Kindly Old Philosopher, "was the President calls in his Secretary of the Treasury.

"'Henry,' he says, frowning, 'I need some more money for my wars on poverty, pollution, pellagra and the Vee-yet-nam-ees. Only we already got taxes on everything from aardvarks to zwieback. We got to think up something to tax that nobody ever thought of taxing.'

"The Secretary shudders. 'Taxes!' he says with a groan.

"'Henry,' says the President, clapping him on the back, 'you're a genius. It's a wonder nobody ever thought of it before.'

"So the President announces a 10 percent surcharge tax on income taxes. A tax tax, that is. And, right off, he drops twenty points in the polls. Folks just don't realize what a great force taxing taxes is going to be in making better men of us all."

I inquired what taxes had to do with character building.

"Why, son," he said, surprised, "taxes are the greatest weapon the Government's got in its unending campaign to run our daily lives, shape our personal destinies and save our immortal souls. Now, you take the high taxes on smoking, drinking and gambling. These days, son, the wages of sin is taxes. Through taxes, the Government's doing its best to save us all from vice. It imposes an amusement tax to keep us home nights, a telephone tax to preserve us from idle chatter, and a gasoline tax to discourage us from driving around in circles.

"And the graduated income tax—there's a blessing. Think of young Horatio Alger. 'If I work hard and persevere,' he says, 'I will reach a bracket where the Government takes 90 percent of my money.' So he loafs on the job, takes it easy and doesn't drop dead at forty of a heart attack. Who knows how many lives this wise tax policy has saved?

"'But be charitable,' says the Government, 'up to 20

percent of Line 15, Page 1. And, seeing suffering is good for your soul, get sick, grow old and go blind. But don't forget to own an oil well.'"

I said I saw his point. But what had the new tax got to do with it?

"Well, son, the Government's been making us virtuous, but it's also been making us a nation of shiftless, unamused, oil-well-owning teetotalers. A dull, stodgy lot. And the President, in his wisdom, sees the need to quicken our lazy minds and stir up our sluggardly mental processes."

But if a tax on alcohol discouraged drinking, then a tax on taxes would merely discourage taxpaying.

"Exactly, son," said the Kindly Old Philosopher with a kindly old triumphant grin. "Don't think of him as taxing our taxes, what he's really doing is taxing our ingenuity."

The Test Tube Babies

How To Come Out Even

Let us pause today in our busy rounds to pay tribute to our men of science and the unending battle they wage to make this old world a better place to live in. Because I think they've been holding their own. Take the Tyler brothers, both eminent in the field of human procreation. Dr. Edward T. Tyler is head of the Tyler Fertility Clinic and, at the same time, president of the American Association of Planned Parenthood Physicians. As you may have read, he's been working on a new fertility pill. And right off the bat, a childless lady produced quadruplets. Which, if you ask me, says a lot about planned parenthood. But if the world owes much to Dr. Edward Tyler, what does it owe his brother, Dr. Albert Tyler of the California Institute of

Technology? For with equal dedication, he has been arduously perfecting an even more smashing breakthrough in the very same field—a vaccine which will keep ladies from getting pregnant.

So in the years to come, there is every hope that millions of human beings will owe to Dr. Ed the very fact they are alive. While millions of others will owe to Dr. Al the very fact they aren't.

You can see what a marvelously balanced program of scientific advance this is. Thanks to the combined efforts of the Tyler brothers, this old world is no worse off than before.

"Yes," you may well say dispiritedly, "but the Dr. Eds have been winning the battle. Thanks to their zeal in stamping out tuberculosis, pellagra and endemic halitosis, we now face the most awful population explosion in the history of mankind."

Have faith in our men of science! cry I. Take courage from the history of our technological age. The invention of the X-ray machine was followed by the invention of the cigarette. New advances in orthopedics were matched by new advances in high-speed automotive engineering. And when all looked bleakest—when infant mortality was virtually eliminated—our dependable men of science came up with Enovid. True, the worst lies ahead. A cure for cancer is, as always, just around the corner. Heart disease is on the run. Each day produces a new advance, wiping out an old scourge.

But cheer up! With the population burgeoning, great

famines are in store. And for every dedicated man of science laboring over his test tube to save human lives and thereby increase the horrors of the population explosion, another sweats over his diagrams of new cobalt bombs, new supersonic missiles, new laser rays—any one of which will lick the problem before you can say, "Take cover!"

So let us pay tribute to our men of science. Due to their untiring efforts, each of us today can look forward to a fruitful life and a happy old age. If they should let us live so long. And let us pay tribute to the scientific credo: "It doesn't matter what you discover as long as it works." For that, I think, is what makes their achievements kind of balance out.

Thus in these crucial times I'm sure the hopes of all of us will go out to our men of science in their unending battle to make this old world a better place to live in. Personally, I just hope they keep on coming out even.

Who Needs the Moon?

Dr. Edward Teller, the Father of the H-Bomb, wishes to blow up the moon to see what it's made of. Actually, he doesn't intend to blow up the whole moon. Just a piece of it. But if he could explode a nuclear bomb on the moon, he says, to see what it's made of . . . And he certainly doesn't think his bomb would blow up the whole moon. He doesn't think.

Of course, Dr. Teller can't blow up the moon without permission. That would be silly. First, he must secure approval from the little-known International Committee for Scientific Tinkering. The Committee, naturally, is composed exclusively of scientists. That's because we laymen don't understand these things. The hearing can only be envisioned.

Scene: The Committee's Project Screening Room. A dozen distinguished scientists are seated in leather chairs about the long, polished oak table.)

Dr. Von Verner: Our next application, gentlemen, is from Dr. Edward Teller. He wishes—let's see here—to blow up the moon.

(There are admiring cries of "What vision!" and "Such broadness of scope!"

Dr. Von Verner (banging his gavel): Decorum, please, decorum. Let us follow established procedure in a proper scientific manner. Now, first, what effects can we postulate from this experiment?

Professor Aston-Martin (working a slide rule): Hmmm, I foresee an interesting global tidal action resulting in a wave approximately 28,763.2-feet high.

Dr. Caligari: Nonsense. The initial effect will be a fascinating shift in gravitational forces. Or, to put it another way, the earth will make a sudden lurch and everybody will fall off.

Dr. Von Verner (rubbing his hands): Good. As long as we have disagreement on anticipated results. After all, there is no point in conducting an experiment if we know how it's going to turn out. Now, if there are no objections . . .

Dr. Yin N. Yang: Excuse me, Doctor, but what about costs? Let's not forget Project Mohole, our magnificent proposal to bore a hole through the earth's crust to see what would leak out. For the lack of a few paltry billion . . .

Dr. Von Verner (frowning): I can't see where blowing up the moon would cost any more than blowing up the Van Allen Belt, and there were no objections to that. (*Nostalgically*) Ah, what a smashing success that was, despite a few miscalculations and surprises.

Dr. Mothersill: No layman objected to that because none knew what the Van Allen Belt was. But I say if we blow up the moon, there's bound to be some public carping. People are going to miss it.

Dr. Von Verner (with a snort): A few songwriters and romantics. It's not their moon, you know. Would they stand in the way of advancing man's knowledge of his environment? How will science ever know what would happen if the moon blows up, unless we blow it up? Let us remember, gentlemen, that our first duty as scientists is to tinker with forces we don't understand until we understand them.

(*The proposal is approved by unanimous acclamation.*)

Dr. Von Verner: Thank you. So much for the moon. Our next project application is from Dr. Jekyll-Hyde of Pomona Teachers College. He offers mathematical evidence that three thermonuclear bombs fired into the sun would create a supernova sufficient to incinerate our galaxy. All for less than $1.2 million. Now then, gentlemen, what is your pleasure?

Uncle of the Z-Bomb

My friend Mrs. Helen Jones, the typical American house-wife, wrote in to say she was watching Dr. Edward Teller, the Father of the H-Bomb, on television the other night. He was, as usual, angrily defending his progeny, as fathers will. Mrs. Jones says she certainly was impressed by his thick, black brows, his penetrating eyes and his suave Central European accent. But she has a question.

"Is it true," she writes, "that Dr. Teller has a castle in Transylvania?"

No, of course not. That's a silly question. Actually, Mrs. Jones is probably thinking of Dr. Edwin Tester, known to a grateful world as "The Uncle of the Z-Bomb." And to his close associates as "that Nut." Dr. Tester does, indeed, have a castle in Transylvania. But due to the pressure of his work, he is only able to visit it once a month. A lunar month. "One has to have a night out to howl," is the way he puts it with a friendly grin which bares his flashing white lateral incisors.

But Dr. Tester devotes the rest of his time to science. He lives simply in a home that is typically American, if sparsely furnished. For it contains nothing but a modest-sized statue of Baal, a box of his native earth on which he sleeps, and a small stone altar. "A scientist has to make sacrifices," he says with a chuckle.

The good doctor is a familiar figure to the neighbors as

he hustles off to work in his secret alchemy lab each evening, astride his white stallion, his black cape swirling around him. What goes on in the secret alchemy lab is, of course, secret. Nor is it for us to ask. For his brilliance in inventing the Z-Bomb cannot be questioned, as he himself has stated on so many television panel shows. The Z-Bomb, as you know, is the ultimate anti-Communist weapon. For a single Z-Bomb, properly detonated, will destroy every Communist everywhere, along with every Communist sympathizer, Commie dupe and fellow traveler. Not to mention all living things.

But as Dr. Tester angrily points out to critics, the Z-Bomb has no blast to depress property values, nor does it leave lingering radiation. "It is an extremely clean bomb," he says irately. "The finest that science can achieve. And it won't hurt a bit."

What makes Dr. Tester maddest, of course is this new treaty which forbids him to test his Z-Bomb. "How can we be certain that it will work without detonating one?" he cries. "And what," he demands, "if the Communists invent a Z-Bomb and kill off every living thing before we can strike back? American must be first," he shouts, "to save the world."

Well, you can't blame Dr. Tester for being mad. How would you like it if most people didn't care much for your offspring? And I'm sure he's a great scientist. But I don't think he's viewing this testing business with what you'd call cool, scientific detachment. In fact, I'd go so far as to say that an angry scientist is a mad scientist.

Which gets us back to Mrs. Jones. I hope I've cleared up her confusion. Dr. Teller is the one who doesn't have a castle in Transylvania.

The Vaterland Makes Its Marks

Good news. The German armaments industry, to which the world is indebted for the military rocket, is at long last manufacturing missiles again. But, the Germans hasten to say, "exclusively for export—especially to underdeveloped countries."

"We see nothing wrong with it," says Herr Joachim Boegner, chairman of the Weapons and Aviation Armament Corporation of Hamburg. "Why should German industry not use opportunities opening up in these countries?"

Why not indeed? And I certainly don't see why the Germans should be so defensive about it. A much more constructive attitude is taken by Baron Himmel von Kreep of nearby South Vaterland. Which as you may recall, is that Central European Republic & Marching Society.

Q—Baron von Kreep?

A—I-have-been-a-lifelong-foe-of-fascism-how-do-you-do.

Q—As chairman of the Von Kreep Peace-loving Munitions Cartel, could you explain your policy of selling missiles to underdeveloped countries?

A—*Jawohl*. It is the duty of all we advanced, prosperous nations to help civilize our poor backward brethren by bringing them the benefits of our modern technology. If the price is right.

Q—Very praiseworthy.

A—*Ach,* true. And every prosperous nation should help the poor in the field in which it excels. You supply them with food, which you produce in surplus. Russia supplies them with Communist dialectics, which it's got too much of. And we supply them with our excellent Vaterland missiles. We will make this a team effort, *ja?*

Q—Wouldn't schools or hospitals be better?

A—Himmel, you idealists! The Vaterland Missiles for Progress program is a practical project. It is the only aid program specifically designed to surmount the one insurmountable problem these poverty-stricken nations all face today.

Q—What's that?

A—Overpopulation.

Q—A noble goal. And I'm sure you could get a better price for your missiles if you sold them to rich nations instead.

A—Well, frankly, with them we often run into a little sales resistance. Take England. Just last week we offered to send forty-seven fine Vaterland missiles a day to London, and all we got back was a two-word cablegram: "NOT AGAIN!"

Q—Yes, I suppose some people will be a bit nervous to hear you Vaterlanders are manufacturing military missiles once more. No offense.

A—But our missiles are exclusively for export.

Q—Exclusively?

A—Exclusively! On my honor as a Vaterlander, I can guarantee that every single rocket we make will be sent outside the border of our beloved Vaterland. Look out the window. Our shipping department is getting ready to export one now.

Q—A very impressive sight.

A—Isn't it? *Achtung!* Ten . . . nine . . . eight . . .

Raise the Anti

"I have called this emergency meeting on national security, gentlemen," said the President gravely, "to discuss the growing missile gap."

"Excuse me, Mr. President," said Dr. Werner von Teller, "it isn't a missile gap precisely. I am proud to say we still have 342 more missiles than they have. The problem is that they are developing anti-missile missiles with which to shoot down our missiles. And while we have more missiles than they, we fear they have more anti-missile missiles. This creates an anti-missile missile gap."

"Did you say 'missile-missile'?" asked the stenotypist, Miss Carbondale.

"No," said Dr. von Teller. "Anti-missile missile." The hyphen comes between the 'anti' and the 'missile.'"

"Thank you," said Miss Carbondale.

"The danger," continued Dr. von Teller, "is that if they perfect an anti-missile that would destroy our missiles, they would then feel free to launch their missiles at us because we have no effective anti-missile missiles."

"Our choice then," said the President, frowning, "is to build either more missiles than they have anti-missile missiles or more anti-missile missiles than they have missiles."

"Excuse me, sir," said Miss Carbondale . . .

"I am anti-missile," said the Secretary of State. "We have a hard enough time now projecting a peaceful image with all the missiles we've got around."

"And I'm afraid I'm anti-anti-missile missile," said the Secretary of Defense, shaking his head.

"Did you say two 'antis,' sir?" asked Miss Carbondale.

"Yes," said the Secretary. "I am against the anti-missile missile. My cost-projection analysis shows that an effective anti-missile missile system would require a capital outlay which breaks down to $97.325 cents per casualty. And that's too high. We need a bigger bang for our buck."

"Well, there's a third alternative," said Dr. von Teller. "With a crash program we could, in a couple of years, perhaps develop a small missile to be carried by our missiles. Thus, when our missiles were attacked by their anti-missile missiles, we could launch these anti-anti-missiles to . . ."

"Pardon me," said Miss Carbondale . . .

"Hold on now," said the President. "That's a dangerous time lag. And what if they're already working on an anti-anti-anti-missile missile missile?"

"Did you say 'missile missile missile,' sir?" asked Miss Carbondale.

"Missile missile," said the President. "But maybe we could build an anti-anti-anti-anti-missile missile. Now, is there anyone present who is anti-anti-anti-anti- . . . Hmmm. Please read that back, Miss Carbondale."

But Miss Carbondale was suddenly seized with a fit of nervous giggling. For some unaccountable reason it spread around the table until even Dr. von Teller was rolling on the floor, clutching his stomach and guffawing, "Anti-anti-anti-anti-anti- . . ."

The very next day the United States proposed a workable treaty for total disarmament.

Some Missiles Are Inscrutable

The news that we are probably going to build an Anti-Chinese Ballistic Missile system (A-CBM) has caused some questions to arise in the public mind, such as: "What the hell's an Anti-Chinese Ballistic Missile?"

This is a good question. The answer, of course, is that an Anti-Chinese Ballistic Missile is not an Anti-Russian Ballistic Missile. And we hope that everyone, particularly the Russians, will understand this clearly drawn distinction. This is crucial because the Secretary of Defense doesn't want to build an expensive Anti-Russian Ballistic Missile system. The Russians, he says, would simply build more Russian Ballistic Missiles, then we'd have to build more antis, which would make them build more . . . And who knows where it would all end? We do, don't we?

So this firm stand makes sense. Unfortunately, we have a lot of generals and such who are just crazy to have an

Anti-Ballistic Missile system of some sort for their very own
—never having had one before. So the Secretary kind of
sighs and says, well, then, let's build a cheap, shoddy, little
system fit only to shoot down cheap, shoddy Chinese missiles. After all, the Chinese are already building missiles
as fast as they can anyway.

But the Russians! Right away they get suspicious and say,
"How do we know your Anti-Chinese Ballistic Missiles won't
shoot down our missiles, too?"

Obviously, we must convince the Russians their missiles
will be safe in making an attack on us. The only conceivable solution is to encourage Russian spies to slip
stealthily into our Anti-Chinese Ballistic Missile factories
and steal the plans for the extraordinary sensory equip-
ment these missiles will employ to distinguish a wily, inscrutable Chinese missile from a husky, stolid Russian one.
This should reassure the Russians that their missiles have
nothing to fear from us. Indeed, it could well lead to the
dawn of a new day of mutual trust:

"There're three hundred thermonuclear missiles passing
overhead, sir," says the Corporal on the Distant Early Warning Line, his finger poised nervously over the Anti-Chinese
Ballistic Missile button. "Are you sure they're Chinese?
They all look alike to me."

"Hold your fire, son," says the Captain, peering through
his binoculars. "They're only Russian friendlies heading
for New York."

Some problems remain to be solved, however. What if
the devious Chinese start building Russian missiles to penetrate our defense system. And if we build Anti-Russian

Ballistic Missiles to counter this threat, what if the Russians should counter-counter with a buildup of Afghanistanian missiles? It's a well-known top secret that we don't have a single Anti-Afghanistanian Ballistic Missile even on the drawing board. Then, if we counter-counter-counter by speeding production of Anti-Afghanis . . .

But let's not get mired down in petty details. After all, in any logical discussion of the inexorable steps inherent in the strategy of nuclear deterrence, we instinctively know where we're all going to wind up. Don't we?

Thou Shalt Not

(*Scene:* The summit of Mt. Sinai.

Time: The present. Moses, holding two stone tablets in his hand, enters nervously.)

Moses: Sorry to bother you again, Sir. But I'm afraid we need another revision in the original copy.

The Lord (with a sigh): Another? What now?

Moses: Well, Sir, it's where You say here, "Thou shall not kill."

The Lord: That seems perfectly clear and concise.

Moses: But it's causing an awful haggle among Your theologians, Sir. The Catholics feel it applies to permatozoa and ova; the Conservatives, only after the union of the two; the Moderates would reserve it for twenty-week-old embryos and up; and the Liberals feel it takes effect precisely at the moment of birth.

The Lord (puzzled): But why would anyone want to kill an unborn child?

Moses: Primarily, Sir, on the chance it might emerge deformed.

The Lord: In that case, why don't they wait to see whether it does before they kill it?

Moses: Oh, all theologians oppose killing children after they're born. Except, of course, at a distance of more than 500 yards.

The Lord: Why 500 yards?

Moses: In wartime, Sir, it is a terrible thing to kill a child with a rifle bullet and an atrocity to do so with a bayonet. But all recognized theologians agree that it is permissible, if regrettable, to blow them up with high explosives or incinerate them with jellied gasoline, as long as it is dropped from an airplane or fired from an artillery piece —particularly, the Christians feel, if you do so to save them from Godless Communism.

The Lord: I suppose it does do that.

Moses: Of course, once a male child reaches the age of eighteen he may be killed in virtually any fashion on the battlefield except with poison gas. The use of poison gas in war, all theologians agree, is the greatest atrocity.

The Lord: Then where do they use it?

Moses: Only in state-operated gas chambers. It is used there, with the approval of theologians, because it is the most humane way to kill people.

The Lord: But if it's the most humane . . . Never mind. Is that all?

Moses: I almost overlooked germ warfare. It is also unconscionable to save people from Godless Communism by inflicting them with any fatal sickness—except radiation sickness, which causes a lingering and painful death.

The Lord (*shaking his head*): Moses, I don't know what to do.

Moses (*briskly*): Well, first off, Sir, I'd suggest setting aside a five-mile stretch of the Pasadena Freeway.

The Lord: Whatever for?

Moses: You certainly aren't going to get the necessary revisions on one of these stone tablets, Sir. Now, I've got a rough draft here of an effective compromise that should mollify all factions. It begins: "Thou shall not kill any person between the ages of minus four months (see Appendix) and eighteen years (asterisk) at a distance of less than 500 yards (see Footnote 7a, Chapter Three), with any of the following . . ."

The Lord (*in measured tones*): Never mind, Moses. I have a better idea. Gabriel? Gabriel, come here. And bring your trumpet.

Psnxtls Will Get Us in the End

I.

A Hole in the Ground

Once upon a time in the Beautiful Green Valley where the wildflowers grew, the Goodguys (who believed in

Wonderfulism) and the Badguys (who believed in Awfulism) decided to talk things over. Because of the fulminous
Psnxtls. As you remember, children, everybody loathed the
dread Psnxtls. But they said they were so terrible-horrible
that no one would ever unleash one. Yet the Goodguys, of
course, had to breed more and more Psnxtls to save the
Valley from Awfulism. And the Badguys, of course, had to
breed more and more Psnxtls to save the Valley from
Wonderfulism. And it was getting so you couldn't go out
to smell a wildflower without stumbling over a slumbering
Psnxtl. They were everywhere.

"We must get rid of the Psnxtls," said the Goodguys.
"Absolutely," said the Badguys. "And we will inspect the
Valley 14½ times a fortnight," said the Goodguys. "No,
11¼!" cried the Badguys. And neither side would back down
for fear of losing face. So they talked and talked. But there
was always hope.

Then the Goodguys discovered that if you dug a hole
in the ground and stuck your head in it, the poisonous breath
of the glominous Psnxtl wouldn't hurt you a bit. "Huzzah!
We are saved!" cried the Goodguys. And they all dug holes
in the ground, shouting the slogan: "Let's Keep Our
Heads!" And, of course, the Badguys saw them do it and
they dug holes in the ground, too. So pretty soon everybody was standing around bent over with his head stuck in
a hole. True, they couldn't negotiate any more. They
couldn't even smell the wildflowers any more. But everybody felt much, much more secure. Indeed, in no time,
everybody was singing "Who's Afraid of the Big Bad
Psnxtl?" And everybody felt braver and braver. In fact, to

show how unafraid they were, people began lashing out with their feet, kicking the silly old harmless Psnxtls to show what they thought of them. And, finally, one woke up!

"Zeeeeeeeee-yowwwwwwwww BOOM!" it roared. And that woke up all the other Psnxtls. And they went on a terrible-horrible rampage. But the holes in the ground worked! Perfectly! Not a single, solitary person was hurt by the poisonous breath of the smolerous Psnxtls. Most of the people were just eaten up alive. Of course, the Psnxtls didn't find everybody. And when the rampage was over, the survivors stood up and brushed themselves off and congratulated each other on how wise they'd been to stick their heads in the ground. And they said: "Now let's get back to the only important thing in the whole Beautiful Green Valley—smelling the wildflowers."

But there weren't any left.

Moral: A good way to lose your head is to stick it in a hole.

II.

The Club Members

Once upon a time in the Beautiful Green Valley where the wildflowers grew, an argument developed over who should be allowed in the Club. There were lots of members. But the Club was really run by the Goodguys, who believed in Wonderfulism, and the Badguys, who believed in Awfulism. That's because they were the only members who bred

Psnxtls—those voracious monsters with gobbly jaws and poisonous breaths rightly feared by one and all. Indeed, they were so frightening that even the Goodguys and Badguys wouldn't take their Psnxtls out for walks, for fear their breath would poison the air, or they would get loose and eat everybody up. So the Beautiful Green Valley dwelt in peace, the wildflowers flourished and all were happy.

All, that is, except for the Terribly Badguys, who believed in the Awfullest Awfulism. They were so awful the Goodguys refused to nod when they passed on the street. And even the Badguys would only say snide and nasty things to them. Which was safe, for the Terribly Badguys didn't have a single Psnxtl to their name. The Terribly Badguys stamped their feet in rage and said, "We're going to breed our own Psnxtls, and when we do we're going to turn them loose to eat up everybody in your stuffy old Club!"

Some members were afraid. But the Goodguys said, "Hmmmph! Psnxtl breeding is a rare art form. Don't worry, it will be twenty years before such backward people as the Terribly Badguys can breed a Psnxtl."

Everyone felt much better, and the Goodguys and the Badguys sat around the Club admiring each other's Psnxtls, chatting about the moon and decrying the Terribly Badguys. In five years, the Terribly Badguys proudly showed off their first Psnxtl.

More members were afraid. But the Goodguys said, "Hmmmmph! It's only a crude little Psnxtl. Besides, they don't have any way to send it anywhere. What good's a Psnxtl you've got to keep at home? Don't worry, it will be ten years before such backward people can perfect a delivery system." And everybody felt much better. The following year, the Terribly Badguys triumphantly showed off their delivery system, complete with Psnxtl.

Just about every member was afraid. But the Goodguys said, "Hmmmmph! It's only a cheap, local delivery system, barely good for sending a Psnxtl next door. Are you going to let those Terribly Badguys force their way into our Club? Don't worry, it will be five years before they can put together a long-distance delivery system and send Psnxtls all the way across the Beautiful Green Valley to eat everybody up."

So everybody felt much better.

Moreover, this time, lo and behold, the Goodguys' prediction proved absolutely right. Almost to the minute.

Moral: Better dead right than dead wrong. But not much.

III.

The Total Victory

Once upon a time in the Beautiful Green Valley where the wildflowers grew, the Goodguys and the Badguys achieved an uneasy peace. Because they were all dreadfully afraid the Psnxtls would get loose. The Goodguys still believed in Wonderfulism. And the Badguys still believed in Awfulism. And each wanted to save the other from what they believed in. But they didn't even throw rocks at each other any more. Because of the dread Psnxtls. The Psnxtls were terribly horrible. They were huge and they had poisonous breaths and fiery eyes and everybody knew that if they got loose, they'd eat everybody up. So the Goodguys and the Badguys dwelt in uneasy peace and the wildflowers grew prettier every year.

Then along came a Brave New Leader of the Goodguys. "To save our Beautiful Green Valley from Awfulism," he cried, "we must win total victory over the Badguys!"

"Hooray," said the Goodguys. "Only," they added nervously, "you're not going to let the dread Psnxtls loose, are you?"

"Of course not," said the Brave New Leader indignantly. "Not, that is, the terribly horrible full-grown Psnxtls. Just a few eensy-teensy baby Psnxtls. Under twelve inches long. After all, they're no worse than conventional rocks."

"But why," asked a cowardly Goodguy, "let any Psnxtls loose at all?"

"Because," said the Brave New Leader, "we've got more baby Psnxtls than they've got. So we will win total victory. And thereby save the Badguys from Awfulism."

And he was absolutely right! The Goodguys unleashed their baby Psnxtls (under twelve inches long), which ate up lots and lots of Badguys, thereby saving them from Awfulism. And the Badguys unleashed their baby Psnxtls (under twelve inches long) which ate up lots and lots of Goodguys, thereby saving them from Wonderfulism. But pretty soon, just as the Brave New Leader predicted, the Badguys ran out of baby Psnxtls (under twelve inches long).

"See!" cried the Brave New Leader triumphantly, "Total victory will now be ours!"

But, unfortunately, the Badguys were unwilling to accept total defeat. In desperation, they unleashed umpteen Psnxtls thirteen and one-half inches long.

"This proves," thundered the Brave New Leader, "that Badguys cannot be trusted. We'll show them a thing or two. Unleash all our Psnxtls up to one yard long."

The Badguys retaliated with a covey of half-grown Psn-xtls, seven feet three inches from snout to tip. The Good-guys, in defense, struck back with . . . Well, anyway, all the Psnxtls inevitably got loose. And inevitably ate everybody up. Thereby saving the Badguys from Awfulism and the Goodguys from Wonderfulism. And thus, as the Brave New Leader predicted, it was a total victory. For both sides. And for the Psnxtls, too.

So everybody was happy. Except maybe the wildflowers, who never did care much for total victory, one way or the other.

Moral: A Psnxtl is a Psnxtl is a Psnxtl.

Part Three
WE, THE WORLD

Friends and Neighbors

The Country That Wanted Love

I.

Dog Eat Dog

Once upon a time there was a big, warm wonderful country. It had towering mountains and shining rivers and fruitful plains and lots and lots of very nice people. It was truly a wonderful country. And what it wanted most of all was to be loved. Like many countries, it had been a bit of a bully at times while growing up. It had picked on smaller countries and pushed weaker people around and even, on occasion, broken its promises. But now that it was full-grown, it didn't want to grow any more. And now that it was rich and powerful, it didn't want to push anybody around any more. It just wanted to be loved. Probably no country ever cared more what other countries thought of it. In order to be loved, it did all sorts of nice things. It gave poorer countries lots of money. It gave weaker peoples lots of help. Above all, it was a very moral country. It never told lies and it always kept its promises. Which is very important if you wish to be loved.

Oddly enough, it was loved. Oh, some older countries said laughingly that it was a little naive and unsophisticated. And some younger countries said enviously it was a little vain and insensitive. But most people thought it was truly a pretty wonderful country. And to many it represented, in quite a real sense, the hope of a better world.

But, of course, now that the wonderful country was rich and strong and full-grown, it had to go out and deal with other countries as an equal. It found that other countries sometimes told lies. And sometimes broke their promises. And were always trying to push you around. In fact, it was kind of a dog-eat-dog world. At first, the wonderful country said this was awful. It would, it said, devote itself to making this a better world by "winning the battle for men's minds." It would teach people to be good by its shining example. And it would never tell lies, break promises or push people around. Because that was the best way to make a better world. But this proved very difficult. And pretty soon, as the wonderful country grew older, it began telling little lies. Like: "That wasn't our spy plane flying over your country." And it began to break its promises. Like: "We pledge never to interfere in the affairs of our neighbors." And it began to push people around.

At first, because it still wanted to be loved, the wonderful country tried to justify what it did. "Golly," it said, "sometimes even we have to lie a little and cheat a little, but it's in a good cause. And when we send our soldiers into other countries, we're doing it for their sakes, not for ours."

But this proved difficult, too. And it became clear the wonderful country would have to choose between being loved and pushing people around. It did. It said: "What's so great about being loved? Who gives a fig what others think? It's a dog-eat-dog world and we've got to be hard-nosed realists and act in our own self-interest." Which worked fine. Because when you act in your own self-interest, you can lie and cheat and push people around all you want. Moreover, with its shining rivers and fruitful plains and nice people, it was still a wonderful country. Of course, it wasn't the hope of the world any more.

Moral: If you have a neighbor who says he doesn't give a fig what other people think of him, count your silverware.

II.

Freedom Is Ringing

Once upon a time there was a great big wonderful nation. It was a wonderful nation because it believed in freedom. Which is why it got into a war in a funny little country half-way around the world.

"Our dear friends, the Whatstheirnames, are in dire peril in the brave little country of Whatchamacallit," said the big country's President. "We shall never rest until they can enjoy the same freedoms we have here at home."

So he sent them a few million bullets, a few thousand dollars and a few dozen soldiers. Some people criticized. "What are we getting into?" they asked. But most applauded. For, after all, freedom is truly worth fighting for. But the generals who ran the little country with a heavy hand kept losing the war. And they spent most of their time quarreling and bopping each other over the head.

"We can't quit now," said the President glumly, "or they'll never enjoy the same freedoms we have here at home." And he sent them a zillion bullets, billions of dollars and a half-million soldiers.

As the war grew, criticism grew. The war, critics said, was illegal, illogical, immoral and just plain stupid.

"In our free society," said the President, who was high in the polls, "we welcome dissent.

"Even though," he added with a frown six months later, "it does prolong the war.

"Thus costing," he mentioned painfully that autumn, "the lives of our boys.

"And does give," he said with a scowl the following spring, "aid and comfort to the enemy.

"Which," he thundered after another three years and $60 billion had gone by, "is the legal definition of treason!"

After that, hardly anybody criticized the war any more. The President was pleased. "With unity," he said, "I can turn my attention to domestic problems."

And he noted that, much as he welcomed dissent, those who would cut his budget were unfortunately prolonging the War on Poverty. While those opposed to his War on Traffic Accidents were "obviously costing the lives of our motorists." And those who grumbled at giving up their summer vacations to dig ditches in his War on Revisionist Agricultural Thinking were "giving aid and comfort to our enemy, the boll weevil."

Thus it was in 1984, as part of the President's War on Costly Political Campaigns, that the President was elected President for life. Of course, the shooting war in the tiny little country halfway around the world still dragged on. But the goal of the great big wonderful country had been achieved. For as the President for Life said, "They now enjoy exactly the same freedoms we have here at home."

And this no one dared deny.

Moral: Freedom is truly worth fighting for. So, in a long, frustrating war don't leave home.

III.

The French Lover

Once upon a time there was a wonderful country called America. It was a very patriotic country. Every American went around saying things like, "My country, right or wrong." And all agreed that no virtue was more praiseworthy than love of one's country. America had lots of friends. One was France. America like France very much. Of course, Frenchmen were oversexed, impractical, supercilious and they'd cheat you blind. And, of course, France was a second-rate, decadent sort of country that had seen better days. But it was an amusing place to visit and they did cook well. So America gave France lots of money when it was poor. And America even let France in its club.

"We are a wonderful country with mighty bombs," said America with a kindly smile. "We'll take good care of you. For old times' sake. You don't have to worry about a thing."

It was a fine arrangement. It proved once again to all Americans what a wonderful country America was. Then along came a big, tall, somber French general with a funny nose. America like the General. He talked a lot about restoring French honor and French glory. "A true patriot," said America approvingly. (For there is no more praiseworthy virtue, as everyone knows, than love of one's country.) Besides, he had a funny nose. So you couldn't take him too seriously. But then the General decided to make a *force de frappe*. Which is kind of a French *bombe* with whipped cream on it.

"What do you want a bomb for?" said America irritably. "We have plenty of bombs already. More than enough to go around. We are a wonderful country. You can count on us to take good care of you."

"The honor and glory of France," said the General stiffly, "demands that we have our own bomb. So that we can take care of ourselves."

The Americans grumbled. But there wasn't much they could do about it. Except to point out in editorial cartoons that the General had a funny nose.

Things went from bad to worse. The General razzed America's friends in Europe. He made snide remarks about America's war in Asia. And he even recognized people America had been cutting dead for years. In the cartoons, his nose got bigger and bigger. The last straw came when the General announced he was withdrawing from America's club. "What!" cried America. "Don't you love us?"

"But I love France more," said the General.

"What!" cried America. "Don't you know we're the most wonderful country in the world?"

"But, no," said the General, surprised. "France is."

Well, there wasn't much America could do. The General's nose was already as big as it could get. So America had to be content with denouncing the General for petty chauvinism.

"It's narrow-minded nationalism like that," said America, shaking his head slowly, "that will ruin the world."

Moral: There is, indeed, no more praiseworthy virtue than love of country. As long as it's yours.

Home of the Free

Those college kids who went to Cuba are raising a big fuss over getting their passports revoked. And I think the problem here is they don't realize this is a free country. You see, Washington says we can't go to Cuba because Cuba isn't a free country like us. And Washington says if we go to Cuba this will be bad for our "security and foreign-policy objectives." Which, of course, aim at keeping our country free. So going to Cuba, they say, isn't good for us.

Now it used to be that Red China was the only country

that wasn't good for us to go to. But the State Department, as years went by, decided to add North Korea. And then North Vietnam. And then Albania. And now Cuba. In order to keep our country free. You can certainly understand this. But has our State Department, I ask, thought things through? Don't be silly.

Take, for example, South Vietnam. Americans go over there and get the idea we're giving $20 million a day to further a dictatorship. They come home and say so. Does this help further our foreign-policy objectives? Of course not. South Vietnam should certainly be added to the list. And Latin America. Here we are trying to promote a Good Neighbor policy. And here are all of us Americans going down there getting drunk, spat on or expropriated. No sir. The only way to promote a Good Neighbor policy is never to drop in on your neighbors at all. So there's another score of countries that are bad for us to go to. As for Africa, you know how touchy things are there. And to let a lot of us fool Americans wander around these new nations shooting off our mouths . . .

"What about Europe?" you say. I agree. Not only do we American tourists add to our gold drain, but our morality's involved. Is it really good for us Americans to visit a country like England? Where Cabinet members chase scantily clad girls around swimming pools? And if the State Department's going to let us go to France, it should at least stamp our passports: "For Adults Only."

But the country that worries me most is East Germany. Do you realize our State Department still lets us Americans travel in East Germany? Which is such an awful dictatorship that it's even got a high wall around it? To keep its oppressed citizens from traveling where they want to? Why, this wall which keeps East Germans from traveling where they want to has become the very symbol of the fact that East Germany isn't a free country! Like us.

So I say our State Department should get on its toes under the slogan: "Today Cuba, Tomorrow the World!" And we can stop all this fuss about passports. Because we Americans won't need them. Meanwhile, I suggest these angry students just remember this is a free country. Where one of our rights has always been to travel where we please. But to keep this a free country with the right to travel where we please, we naturally have to give up certain rights. Like traveling where we please.

It behooves all of us in these times to help Our Leaders preserve our precious freedoms. By giving them up. One by one. Or, as my friend Miss Amanda puts it: "Anybody who says this isn't a free country should be clapped in jail!"

Peace Through Greed

Tidings of joy! World peace is just around the corner. Again. Oh, I know idealists have been preaching peace through love, charity and brotherhood for years. And it hasn't worked out too well. But now we've got a new approach. And I'm brimming over with faith. It involves bread. As you know, we've got surplus wheat coming out of our silos. And, as you know, a lot of people in Communist countries are very hungry. But we won't sell them our wheat because we wish to save them from Communism. Even if we have to starve them all to death to do it. This has long been the cornerstone of our foreign policy. But then Canada and Australia (those rat finks) went and sold wheat to Russia. What an outcry in Congress! Especially by our militantly anti-Communist Congressmen from the Midwest.

"This is no time for Pollyana platitudes," outcried Senator Carlson of Kansas for one. "World trade is a cold and calculated business operation." And how come, he said militantly, his constituents can't sell their wheat to Russia too?

So it looks now as though we may make a deal with the Communists: money for bread. And then, naturally, they won't be quite so ready to blow up the hand that feeds them. And then, naturally, we'll think twice before incinerating a profitable market. And both sides will be more inclined to live in peace. Here at last is a path we can follow with confidence. Here at last is an emotion in which we can have faith. For greed, unlike love, charity and brotherhood, is universal. Greed transcends national boundaries, it is shared by rich and poor, it stands above petty politics. And already you can foresee a brave new world in which we and the Communists peacefully stroll side by side into a golden future. With our hands in each other's pockets.

But, unfortunately, greed has been a much-maligned emotion over the years. It's got a bad image. And if we are going to achieve peace through greed, we will need the best efforts of our best citizens to re-educate the public. Liberals should immediately unite as one in such groups as "Women

for Greed," "Turn Toward Greed" and "The National Committee for a Greedy Foreign Policy." Conservatives may
contribute to "The National Association of Greedy Manu-
facturers" or their local Chamber of Avarice. On the other
hand, we needn't worry about converting the leaders of the
Radical Right. After all, they've been making money out of
Communism for years.

Of course, we may meet public resistance. You know
how hard it is to put over these idealistic do-good campaigns.
And maybe it would be easier simply to tell ourselves we are
selling food to these hungry people out of love, charity and
brotherhood. Indeed, I'm sure we will.

Sticks and Stones

Following is another chapter in that standard unpublished
reference work *A History of the World, 1950–1999.* The
title of this unwritten chapter is "Civilization and Who
Needs It?"

Early in the year 1967, the United States embarked on
a radical new foreign policy. It was best summed up by the
chairmen of both the Senate and House Armed Services
Committees, who said, in separate statements, that America
ought to bomb whomever it wanted to bomb and, as one of
them put it, "Let world opinion go fly a kite." Editorial
writers, retired generals and other evangelists picked up the
cry and the phrase "Who cares what others think?" was on
every lip—especially thrust-forth lower lips. In the White

House plans were laid for another invasion of Cuba. This time with adequate air cover.

After centuries of the Puritan ethic and narrow moral restrictions, the new philosophy struck a responsive chord in the American breast. The first documented evidence of this came when Mr. Homer T. Pettibone, an advertising copywriter, showed up for work on Madison Avenue wearing a tattersall vest, a fat Max tie and tennis shoes. Moreover, he ordered a chocolate malt, rather than three martinis, for lunch. "I like chocolate malts better," he said defiantly. "And who cares what others think?" Although Mr. Pettibone was promptly sacked, the mood spread. A week later, a Peoria pushcart peddler was arrested for removing his trousers because he was hot.

But the incident that unleashed the tide was the finals of that year's Miss America Beauty Pageant. Instead of breaking into smiling tears on hearing that she had lost, runner-up Betty Mo Meridee screamed, "I was robbed!", hiked her skirt and kicked the winner, Miss Sharalee Shnipes—smack on nationwide television.

The rest was inevitable. The City Council of Appalachia Corners scraped up enough money to send all the local poor to Trenton, New Jersey, by bus, where they qualified for relief. Church attendance fell, marriages dissolved and no one ventured on the highways, as it was quickly discovered that a healthy respect for the opinions of other motorists, particularly at busy intersections, was all that had kept traffic fatalities in the five-figure bracket. With society not caring what society thought, manners and morals crumbled. Householders barricaded themselves in their homes.

And it was a sad day when the chairman of the House
Armed Services Committee was waylaid by one of the gangs
of toughs who now roamed the streets, robbing, raping and
looting.

"This is outrageous!" he sputtered.

"Who cares," said the gang leader, flicking open a switch-
blade, "what you think, pops?"

As for world opinion, it came to the conclusion that
America had descended into barbarism. And while the world
may have been right, Americans were too busy defending
their lives and their homes from each other to care very
much.

Our Sacred Commitments

The Middle East Crisis has stimulated some public interest in our Sacred Commitments. Many informed citizens
were mildly surprised to learn that several of our Presidents,
including the incumbent, had made Sacred Commitments
to defend not only the territorial integrity of Israel, but also
that of Egypt, Jordan, Syria, Lebanon and other nations.
Like Vietnam, Laos, Thailand . . .

So, in order to clarify any lingering confusion in the
public mind, I dropped over to the National Archives of
Sacred Commitments in the basement of the Washington
Monument for a chat with its curator, Dr. Homer T. Pettibone, D.V.M. I found Dr. Pettibone happily surrounded by
stacks upon stacks of Sacred Commitments of all shapes, sizes

and degrees of yellowed age. I said I was surprised to find that the Archives contained more than one kind of Sacred Commitment.

"Oh, they come in hundreds of different varieties," said Dr. Pettibone polishing his pince-nez. "But we file them under three general headings: Very Sacred Commitments, Plain Old Sacred Commitments, and Casual Sacred Commitments."

Could he explain the difference?

"Surely," he said, reverently drawing forth an impressive one labeled "NATO Agreement."

"Now here is a Very Sacred Commitment. As you can see, our President pledges us to go to war in behalf of a whole passel of countries in Western Europe. Naturally, under our Constitution, this treaty had to be ratified by the Senate after long and solemn debate over the wisdom of making such a grave promise."

"Naturally," I said. And what did a Plain Old Commitment look like?

"Well, here's one," he said, pulling out a letter addressed, "To the Premier of Vietnam Whom It May Concern."

"As you can see, a Plain Old Commitment is a letter or public statement made by a President to go to war for somebody if asked."

But if both kinds pledged the Nation to go to war, what was the difference?

"I thought I explained that," said Dr. Pettibone irritably. "The first kind is ratified by the Senate.

"Now here," he continued, flicking on a tape recorder, "is a Casual Sacred Commitment."

A familiar voice said, "And if there's anything we can ever do for you, you just ask."

"Now, let's see," said Dr. Pettibone, frowning, "did he say that to the Ambassador for Upper Volta at a garden party or the Foreign Minister of Outer Mongolia over root beer? We really should know so that we don't go to war with the wrong country."

"My," I said, "we certainly had a lot of Sacred Commitments."

"Oh, we have Sacred Commitments," said Dr. Pettibone with a true curator's pride, "with countries you never heard of."

And would we honor them all?

"Like any great nation with its honor at stake, we stand ready when the time comes to keep sacred each and every one of our Sacred Commitments," said Dr. Pettibone with dignity, "that we can't get out of."

L.B.J.'s Good Resolutions

Herewith is another unwritten chapter in that unpublished reference work *A History of the World, 1950–1999.* The title of this chapter is, "The Resolutionary War."

It was on a stormy night in August of 1964 that several torpedo boats of unconfirmed nationality reportedly attacked a couple of American destroyers in the Gulf of Tonkin without any damage. The President said this was an insult to our flag and asked the Senate for permission to get even. The

Senators in a burst of patriotic furor hastily passed a resolution advising the President that he certainly should do just that.

To show these torpedo boats that the U.S. meant business, the President launched daily all-out air attacks on North Vietnam, which is handy to the Gulf of Tonkin, and dispatched half a million troops to South Vietnam in the event the torpedo boats should strike at that defenseless nation. Three years and $50 billion passed. Some Senators grew uneasy. "Haven't those torpedo boats been sunk yet?" one wanted to know. And several went so far as to say publicly that they hadn't meant for the President to get *that* even.

The President took the criticism good-naturedly. He even sent an emissary to Capitol Hill to remind the Senators of the historic American doctrine of "advise and consent."

"The President advises you all to shut up," said the emissary, "and consents to go on getting even his way."

The Senators, their dignity wounded, angrily passed a second resolution rescinding the Gulf of Tonkin Resolution.

"That will make the President withdraw from this inane war," said Senator Fulbright, rubbing his hands.

Instead, the President promptly announced the bombing of Hanoi "under authority granted me by Senate Resolution 1435 unanimously adopted in 1947."

This resolution turned out to be one urging "wide-scale urban renewal." The Senators, now furious, immediately rescinded it, too. The President, however, continued the war, successively citing Senate resolutions favoring World Travel Week (1953), Hands Across the Sea Day (1927) and Manifest Destiny (1898). The Senate rescinded them as fast as he cited them.

At last the President announced he was sending another half-million troops to Vietnam, "because," he said with a jolly wink, "you know how our fine boys behave in foreign lands." And this time he cited Senate Resolution 2371 of 1936—a Mother's Day resolution praising motherhood as "the greatest of God's gifts." Despite a long and bitter debate, the Senators couldn't bring themselves to vote against motherhood.

"I'm mighty pleased," said the President. "It would be unconstitutional for me to wage war without the approval of our fine Senators. So let us continue to press forward with resolution—whichever one happens to be handy."

Thus the war dragged on. It was never recorded what happened to those torpedo boats.

The Great Big Bull

I.

The Nervous Nellies

Once upon a time there was a Great Big Bull who led his herd into a quagmire. It could happen to anybody. But in his mighty struggles to get them out he managed only to sink them all in deeper. A few members of the herd—mostly rebellious young calves—questioned the Great

Big Bull's judgment. Some thought they ought to go back the way they'd come and some were for charging off to the right or to the left or whichever. At first, the Great Big Bull smiled tolerantly at this small minority. "It is a tribute to the democratic way I run this herd," he said, "that I allow these well-intentioned but misguided critics to speak out at a time like this. Now let us struggle on."

So the herd struggled on, floundering and thrashing about. And pretty soon they were all in up to their knees.

"Maybe we ought to stop for a minute to get our bearings," a bespectacled bull named Nellbright suggested somewhat hesitantly. For all members of the herd were understandably afraid of the Great Big Bull.

"You have the inalienable right in this herd to suggest anything you want," said the Great Big Bull testily. "Even though you are obviously blind to experience, deaf to hope and are perhaps giving aid and comfort to the quagmire. Now let us struggle on!"

So the herd struggled on, floundering and thrashing about. And pretty soon they were all in up to their bellies.

"I know we are the mightiest and most powerful herd in the world," said the bespectacled bull named Nellbright with a worried frown. "But it seems to me our struggles are merely getting us in deeper."

This made the herd a little uneasy. "Nobody," snorted the Great Big Bull, "wants to get out of this quagmire more than I. Now let us struggle on!"

So the herd struggled on, floundering and thrashing about. And pretty soon they were all in up to here.

"We must tie a rope around our necks and all pull to-

gether," ordered the Great Big Bull. "Straight ahead, now
. . . two . . ."

"But if we go that way," protested the bespectacled bull
named Nellbright, "we'll all go right over the . . ."

"Listen, you Nervous Nellie," bellowed the Great Big
Bull, frustrated beyond endurance, "you're trying to pull us
apart to promote yourself. Anybody who turns on his own
leader, his own herd, is a Nervous Nellie. Now, to preserve
our democratic way of life, everybody shut up, pull together
and follow me."

And it worked! The herd, not wishing to be thought
Nervous Nellies by the Great Big Bull, shut up, pulled together and blindly followed their leader—out of the quagmire, up a small rise, and right over an 8000-foot cliff.

Moral: Silencing criticism in a democracy requires a lot
of bull.

II.

The Loyal Opposition

Once upon another time, a Great Big Bull led his herd
into a mire.

"Don't worry," he said confidently. "I did it on purpose.
I have calculated that if we all tread together very carefully,
we can stomp out this muck and create a beautiful green
pasture where everyone can graze in peace. All together,
now. But gently. For if we stomp too hard the sky will fall
down."

So the herd, without much thinking, did what the Great Big Bull said. And pretty soon they were all in up to their fetlocks.

"It is obvious," said the Great Big Bull with a frown, "that we must gradually increase the pressure to conquer this mire. All together, now. A bit harder."

And pretty soon the herd was in up to its knees.

"Thrash around!" cried the Great Big Bull. "But not too hard. We don't want the sky to fall down."

And pretty soon the herd was in up to its withers. At this point there was a lot of grumbling. And a minority of the herd got together in one corner of the mire to talk over what could be done.

"We must support our leader in this hour of crisis," said a big white-maned bull named Everett, who had cowlike eyes and a soft, lowing voice. "For politics stops at the mire's edge. Or does anyone have a better idea?"

"I say we should thrash around harder, conquer this mire and get the hell out!" said a crusty old bull scarred from many a battle.

"Hush," said Everett nervously. "You will frighten the cows and the calves. We certainly don't want to lose their support."

"I say," said a handsome young bull, "that we should very gingerly and delicately extricate ourselves from this mire and withdraw to safer ground."

"What!" said Everett, "and publicly abandon all hope of creating a beautiful green pasture? Why, we would risk being hooted out of the herd as cowards and defeatists."

"But the Great Big Bull made a terrible mistake leading us into this mire," protested one bull.

"True," everyone said, nodding sagely.

"And the Great Big Bull is clearly doing the wrong thing by thrashing around," said another.

"That's right," everyone said, nodding sagely.

"But let's not sound disloyal," said Everett. "It would cast discredit on us."

"You can't deny that," everyone said, nodding sagely.

So, after a great deal of thinking, the minority group finally composed a policy statement, which was read to the entire herd. It said:

"The Great Big Bull, after making a series of terrible mistakes, is following a course that is bound to lead to disaster, and we support him 100 percent."

The herd broke into applause at this grand display of both wisdom and loyalty, two cherished virtues. The herd was reassured. The Great Big Bull was encouraged to go on thrashing. And none was happier than Everett.

"We have won the full support of the herd for our responsible program combining wisdom and loyalty," he said, holding his head high. "And surely nothing is more important than that."

He probably would have had more to say, as he was a great talker. But, unfortunately, he couldn't hold his head high any longer and he, along with the rest of the herd, disappeared under the muck.

Moral: Wisdom and loyalty are both admirable virtues. It's too bad you usually have to make a choice.

The Ruler Who Wanted Love

Once upon a time there was an old king who wanted to be loved. He wanted to be loved more than anything else in the world. When he became king he did everything he could to make the people love him. He helped the poor and educated the ignorant and cured the sick and spread all the largesse he could throughout the land. He even sent forth his wife, the queen, to beautify the countryside. And, oh, how the people loved him. And, oh, how happy he was.

Unfortunately, however, the country became involved in a little war in a little land far, far away. The king, basking in the love of his people, said confidently not to worry, he would lead them to a glorious and easy victory. And the people, loving and believing in him, cheered lustily.

But the little land far, far away, unbeknownst to the king, lay under an all-entangling magic spell. No matter how many soldiers or how much gold the king poured into the war, he couldn't win it. And, being proud, he couldn't lose it. Moreover, and worse yet, he couldn't afford it.

The people grew uneasy. The king grew desperate.

"Victory is just around the corner," he said. Which wasn't true.

"Anybody who doesn't love this war doesn't love our country," he said. Which wasn't true.

Pretty soon, most of the country's young men and most of the country's gold were gone. The people didn't believe anything he said any more. And, worst of all, nobody loved him. He couldn't leave his castle, except in the dead of night under heavy guard, for fear the people would stone him. And young knights and courtiers and robber barons hatched plots to seize his crown.

Well, one day, the old king was sitting all alone on his throne, his head in his hands. "Oh," he cried from his heart, "I would give up anything I possess for the secret of how to be loved again."

A good fairy passing by heard his cry, took pity on him and whispered the secret into his ear. The very next day, to everyone's surprise, the old king renounced the throne. It hurt him deeply to hear how the people cheered and to see how they threw their caps in the air. "We're rid of him at last!" they shouted happily as he squnched his shoulders. But as time passed and the young knights and courtiers and robber barons squabbled among themselves for his crown, and as the war dragged on even without him, the mood of the people slowly changed.

Nobody attacked the old king any more, for he was without power. Nobody questioned his decisions any more, because he didn't make any. And nobody envied him his crown, because he didn't have one. The people remembered the good things he'd done and forgot his mistakes. They laughed at his sallies and applauded his crustiness and began to venerate him as "an elder statesman."

In fact, they came to love him again.

And, as that was what the old king wanted more than anything else in the world, he lived happily ever after.

In the Back Yard

A Gringo's Guide

In response to popular demand, herewith is another chapter of that unfinished reference work *An American's Guide to Foreign Lands*. This one is called, "Latin America—An Enigma."

Latin America is a hot, dirty area south of Tijuana. It is about the size of New Jersey. You cannot drink the water. But it's a nice place to visit if you can't afford to go to Europe. The people are illiterate, gay, poor, friendly, apathetic, happy and always stirring up revolutions. We are the best friend they have. We feel sorry for them.

Actually, Latin America is a lot of little countries. They are called "Our Sister Republics." In the interests of Western Hemisphere solidarity, we are always very careful to address Our Sister Republics as equals. Even though we can never remember their names. The only country that is

not Our Sister Republic is Cuba. That's because Cuba
tries to export guns and revolutionaries to Our Sister Republics. This is unethical, underhanded and an unwarranted
interference in the internal affairs of other countries. Such
acts cannot be tolerated. That's why we ship guns and revolutionaries to Cuba. In addition, Cuba is run by a dictator
and the people are not free. That is why its government must
be overthrown. All the dictators of Our Sister Republics
agree with us on that.

Not all Our Sister Republics are run by dictators, however. Some are run by military juntas. They are called in
Washington "a force for stability." We are against stability.
We are for "rapid social change." That's because in Latin
America we are "sitting on the edge of a volcano." The
reason for this is that there are two classes of people in
Our Sister Republics—the downtrodden peons in whom
burns bright the flame of freedom, and the ruling officials,
all of whom are corrupt.

To produce rapid social change we formed the Alliance
for Progress. It is a partnership of equals. In return for our
pledge to give them $20 billion, the officials agreed to ac-
cept it. So far it hasn't done the peons much good. Nobody knows why. But at least we have come a long way
since the days of "Gunboat Diplomacy" when we sent battleships and Marines to force our will on Our Sister Republics. That was last year.

Thus we see the challenge we face today in Latin America: We must staunchly support the beloved, corrupt, stable
governments of Our Sister Republics while helping the
ignorant, lazy, freedom-loving peons kick them out of office.

Yet we are vigorously opposed to intervening forcefully in their affairs. Unless we can't think of anything else.

This is called "Our Good Neighbor Policy." At heart it means that they can count on us, their Big Brother, never to forget the special ties that bind us to Our Sister Republics to the south. Whatever their names are.

Yes, We've Got No Dictators

Our Alliance for Progress, which aims at social reform in Latin America, is certainly making progress. In a way. Hardly a billion dollars goes by that some government down there doesn't get reformed. By its Army. I'd like to explain this phenomenon, but I'm not an expert on any of our Latin American neighbors. So I've had to invent one. It's a lovely little independent republic known to our State Department as "Cosa Nostra."

Cosa Nostra lies just south of the docks and has a population of 3,000,073. Of which 42 are peons, 41 are soldiers and the rest are bananas. For years and years it was governed peacefully by General Cosa (The Ogre) Nostra. And there was never a complaint. Not from the General, who was happy. Nor from the soldiers, who were happy. Nor from the peons. Who knew what was good for them. But things got more and more revolting until finally the peons revolted. The Army gave up without firing a shot. Mainly because their 1812 muskets all failed to go off. General Nostra fled into exile (after stopping at the bank). And a

President whose name we never could remember was elected and began a vigorous program of social reform.

But then Castroism raised its ugly beard. In Cuba. Our State Department was alarmed. "We must save Cosa Nostra from Castroism!" cried Washington. The Alliance for Progress was launched. We sent 113 experts to Cosa Nostra to determine what was needed to stem the tide of Castroism.

"Well," says El Presidente Whatshisnombre, "we could use food, teachers, books . . ."

"Great, great," says our Ambassador. "But look at that raggedly-old bobtail army you've got. How do you expect to defend democracy with an army like that? We will include in our first shipment 474 tanks, 362 jet fighters and a couple of used battleships. Take your time in paying us back."

So at the bargain rate of only a billion or so, we managed to reform the Cosa Nostra Army into a modern, superbly equipped fighting force. And, oh, how happy the soldiers were to lay down their 1812 muskets. And pick up their brand-new burp guns.

"Hey, man!" cried the tank drivers in the turrets of their streamlined U.S. tanks. "Look at these hot rods go." And with that they rolled right over the Presidential Palace. Not to mention El Presidente Whatshisnombre.

General Cosa (The Ogre) Nostra returned from exile and took over. On the grounds he was more against Castroism than anybody. Which our State Department had to admit was certainly true. And, once again, there are no complaints in Cosa Nostra. Not from the General, who feels more secure. Nor from the soldiers, who love their burp guns. Nor from the peons. Who, after all, don't wish to complain against tanks, jet fighters and battleships.

So the Alliance is making Progress. Every week, it seems, we produce another highly stable government supported by an awesome army—an ally strong and powerful enough to defend forever the principles of democracy. If it had any.

El Beejay Makes Peace

Once upon a time there was a country called America. It was having a Civil War. The Government was fighting the Rebels. The Rebels were winning. And then another country, called the Dominican Republic, landed 100,000 Marines at Coney Island.

"We are here," explained their leader, General El Bee-jay, with a benevolent smile, "solely to protect the lives and property of Dominican citizens. We are here merely to make peace. As for your Civil War, we are completely impartial and don't give a hoot which side wins. As long as it's the Government's."

The Rebel leader, General Robert P. Lee, said he loved all Dominicans. But why didn't they go make peace somewhere else? The Government leader, General Ulysses F. Grant, figured anything was better than losing. Even Dominican peacemakers. At first all went well. The Dominican Marines, being better trained, better equipped and better paid, drove the Rebels back on all fronts. "We merely wish to protect Dominican property now in Rebel-held territory," explained General El Beejay. "Charge, men!" he would shout to his troops while waving his sword over his head. "And I sure do hope nobody gets hurt."

General Grant was delighted with the string of victories this gave him. But he didn't care for the constant stream of advice General El Beejay kept offering, such as: "Attack their left flank!" "Make your cavalry charge now!" and "You drink too much."

At last, it was more than General Grant could bear. And he arranged a meeting with General Lee at a place called Appomattox to talk things over. "Bob," said General Grant, "what do you think of these here Dominicans now?"

"Well, Ulysses," said General Lee, "to tell the truth I don't love them as much as I used to. Mainly because they keep trying to shoot my head off."

"You should have them on your side, Bob," said General Grant with a wary sigh. "Nag, nag, nag. They don't speak our language or understand our ways. And my boys are complaining that they get all the girls."

"Well, you know these high-handed foreigners," said General Lee. "Un-American busybodies," agreed General Grant. And after a couple of drinks and a little more talk, General Lee and General Grant signed the Treaty of Appomattox, ending the Civil War right on the spot.

To this day, historians credit General El Beejay's intervention not only for ending the Civil War, but also for unifying every American man, woman and child as they had never been unified before. Of course, what they were unified in was the new war jointly declared that night by Generals Grant and Lee on the Dominican Republic.

Moral: Blessed are the peacemakers; for they shall be called the children of God. Among other things.

The Ratt of Phynkia

Herewith is another unpublished chapter in that unpublished textbook *A History of the World, 1950–1999.* This chapter is entitled "The Ratt of Phynkia."

The Johnson Doctrine, proclaimed in the 1960s, banned the staging of any unauthorized revolutions in any hemisphere. And by the early 1970s, American troops were engaged in antiguerrilla warfare in forty-three nations on six continents. It was at this critical point that trouble broke out in Phynkia, a small oasis 420 miles southeast of Khartoum as the camel crawls. Phynkia (populated 37) was governed by a hereditary ruler or "Ratt," who was invariably corrupt, despotic, sadistic, grumpy and anti-Communist. He thus qualified for American aid and the title "A Leader of the Free World."

In the spring of 1973, the current Ratt got in a fight with his brother-in-law over whose turn it was to use the Bentley. The Ratt appealed for American troops to preserve his "bastion of democracy," and a C.I.A. agent was dispatched to investigate. The agent quickly determined that the brother-in-law had neither signed a loyalty oath nor even made a preliminary application to the State Department for permission to revolt. Moreover, his report said, the populace supported their ruler, as evidenced by their daily custom of lining up in front of the palace and chanting, "Ratt, Phynkia . . . Ratt, Phynkia . . ."

Back in Washington, the President went on network television to announce that "as Phynkia goes, so goes whatever else is around wherever it is." And he ordered "all available military aid" sent to the Ratt.

The last troops remaining on American soil were dispatched, and it was a tearful scene when his mother bade him farewell. On landing in Phynkia, the last troops, whose name was Corporal Homer T. Pettibone, handed out chewing gum to the kids and called for "close air support." For this crucial mission, the Strategic Air Command decided to throw in "every uncommitted aircraft." This turned out to be a deHaviland biplane with a myopic pilot who, through "a navigation error," dropped his bombs smack on Phynkia itself, thus blowing the Ratt, his brother-in-law and all other thirty-five Phynkians to smithereens.

The President went on television to announce proudly that American military might had once again saved a nation from unauthorized revolution. "Let this be an example to our allies," he said, "that they can count on us."

At that moment, unfortunately, sixteen Mexican wetbacks crossed the Rio Grande, and, finding no opposition, took California. New York, which had been without electricity, newspapers or running water for three years, surrendered to two troops of Boy Scouts on tour from Luxembourg. Washington lay defenseless and was quite miffed to discover no one wanted it. Weeks of turmoil followed. Finally, "as a gesture of friendship," Costa Rica dispatched a regiment of Marines to "prevent an unauthorized revolution."

The Costa Rican colonel went on network television to promise the American people that "free elections will be held as soon as conditions warrant."

They never did.

Brotherhood Way

They Call It U.N.

Once upon a time there was an organization with the unlikely name of "The U.N." It was staffed by people with such unlikely names as "U Thant" and "Odd Bull." And its purpose was "to keep the peace." Which was the most unlikely thing about the whole unlikely organization.

The members of the U.N. were always willing to dump any crisis in its lap—any crisis, that is, that they couldn't see any likelihood of solving through devious diplomacy, threats of force or the usual power politics. Consequently, this unlikely organization dealt only with crises where solutions looked unlikely. And its method of solving them was the unlikeliest method the world had ever seen.

Each member would get up and say that he was wholeheartedly for peace, that peace could only be achieved through a spirit of fair play and mutual understanding, and that the other side was a bunch of liars, cheats and no-good rat finks. That done, they'd all adjourn to the Members Lounge, have a beer and settle the whole thing privately. And you couldn't ask for a more unlikely method than that. But as the U.N. grew into more than one hundred members, it naturally took longer for everybody to castigate everybody else as rat finks. Consequently, it took longer to adjourn to the Members Lounge and settle a crisis privately.

Finally, a crisis came along that took the U.N. a whole week to settle. For days, the members debated who were the biggest rat finks. It got so it took an hour of angry talk to decide whether to adjourn for ten minutes. Eventually, the weary members got to the Members Lounge, where they quickly agreed on a demand for a cease-fire and how to police it. But by that time, world opinion had at last turned against the U.N. "That isn't just unlikely," said exasperated television viewers, switching in disgust to I Love Lucy. "It's unbelievable."

So the U.N. was abolished, and the very next crisis was solved in believable, likely fashion. Country X got into a fight with Country Y, which had always been likely. The other countries lined up in two armed camps and called each other liars, cheats and rat finks, as they are always likely to do. This time, however, nobody adjourned to the Members Lounge to agree privately on a cease-fire, there being no Members Lounge to adjourn to. Not that it mattered, for there was no one to order a cease-fire and no one to police it. So both sides kept on firing until, of course, they blew up the world.

But as the few survivors agreed, in a tension-ridden thermonuclear age, you couldn't ask for a more likely solution than that.

Moral: The only thing that keeps mankind going is an unlikely hope things will get better. But there's nothing wrong with that if you consider the likely alternative.

Family Fun

It's the season for indoor games. And I'm glad to note there's lots of new fun games for grownups and kiddies alike this year, such as *Summit, Stratego, Tactics, Risk* and *Victory Over Communism.* The object of most of these new fun games, of course, is to see who can conquer the world first. They have much in common: a map of the world, markers, a pair of dice and a set of very complicated rules. Most also boast they "realistically reflect" the struggles of international diplomacy. This is a downright lie and a fraud on the public. Actually, the only fun game which realistically reflects the struggles of international diplomacy is the one I happen to have invented myself. It's called: *Look Out! Look Out!* comes complete with a map of the world, a thick rule book and two heavy clubs. The clubs are issued to the two biggest players, who are then known as "Power Blocs." The rest of the players are called "Neutrals." They don't do anything.

The rule book is terribly important. Each player is required to memorize it from cover to cover. The rules include Respect for Territorial Integrity, Freedom of the Seas, Peaceful Settlement of Disputes, and Not Clobbering Anybody Unless He Clobbers You First. Obviously, these rules make it impossible for any player to conquer the world. Thus, each player progresses only by breaking the rules. Let's say the first Power Bloc decides to violate Territorial Integrity. He stands up, whirls his club around his head and plops down on top of the nearest Neutral. All the other players then cry, "Look Out!" Each takes turns citing at the top of his lungs which rule has been violated. (This shows you the importance of knowing the rules.) In response, the first Power Bloc shouts "Self defense!" and "National Interest!" as loudly as he can until everybody's tired of the whole thing. It's then the other Power Bloc's turn to play.

Eventually, of course, one Power Bloc accidentally steps on the other Power Bloc's toes. Or unintentionally gouges him with an elbow. The other Power Bloc is then entitled to smack the first Power Bloc with his club. This signals a general melee in which the game room is reduced to shambles. The first player who demolishes the map of the world is declared the winner. Because once the world is demolished, naturally, this fun game is over.

For those who don't care for quite such a realistic, exciting game, I've invented another. It's called *Peace*. Its only object is to leave well enough alone. Each player, as long as he doesn't bother any other, may move as he sees fit—such as by reading a book, watching television or going for a walk in the woods to smell the rain-wet grass.

But, frankly, there isn't much of a market for it. I suppose the basic trouble is Peace isn't much fun. No sir, there's a deep yearning in all game players for the joys of strategy, tactics and conquest. And I've got the answer: *Look Out!*

The Spirit of Glassboro, New Jersey

Summit conferences, as you know, produce good or bad spirits—such as the Spirit of Vienna (bad) or the Spirit of Camp David (good, but ephemeral). Assuming that commentators are going to be talking about the Spirit of Glassboro, New Jersey, in coming years, I thought you might want to know what it was like.

"Have a cup of cold water, son," the big volunteer fireman said to a perspiring reporter as he hefted up a five-gallon jug on the lawn outside the summit meeting. "It'll do you good. Our water's naturally fluoridated. Comes from artesian wells that go down 805 feet. We got studies showing . . ."

You can see right off that the Spirit of Glassboro is warm, hospitable and perhaps a little talkative. But there's nothing wrong with that.

"I guess this is about the most exciting thing that's happened around here," said a tiny, elderly man with thick glasses, "since the junior-mechanics building burned down back in 1945. Or was it '46? Let's see, my daughter was about four then and . . ."

So it's a quiet spirit, family oriented and deeply rooted in the past. It's devout, too.

"Is this historic?" a frail lady of seventy or so asked, tugging a reporter's sleeve.

"I guess so, ma'am," he said.

She thought for a moment. "I think, then," she said, mostly to herself, "that I should pray."

But it's very progressive.

"We have a big urban-renewal program going and some elderly housing, too," said Mr. Robert Wallace, a former councilman who hung a sign on the door of his appliance store on summit day saying, "Gone to see the Pres."

"It isn't like nothing ever happens here. We've got two bowling alleys and a movie. And we had the biggest parade you ever saw for the New Jersey Tercentenary three years ago. Then the college baseball team just took second in the national championships and the high-school track team . . ."

"The high school's got the first outdoor aluminum grandstand in the country," proudly said Mr. George Beach, a member of the Board of Education. "No, we don't have any marijuana or anti-Vietnam parades or things like that. Not much violence at all."

"A guy cut himself slicing cheese down at the grocery last Friday night," said a young policeman, laughing.

But the spirit is also thoroughly independent.

"The Governor can have the President and the Premier come to my house and I'm delighted," the wife of Glassboro State College President Thomas E. Robinson was quoted as saying while workmen shoved her furniture around in preparation for the momentous event, "but nobody's going to look in my ice box."

And so it was that Mr. Kosygin emerged from his first

long session with Mr. Johnson and stood for a moment on
an embankment under the leafy oaks and dogwood looking
down on the roped-off crowd of perhaps 1000 Glassboroans
below. They caught sight of him and cheered—nuns, teen-
agers, balloon and ice cream salesmen, everybody cheered
and waved their signs for peace. He made a short speech
saying he was for peace, too. And though no one could understand a word he said, they all cheered wildly again,
smiling and grinning and applauding. The spirit was heavy
in the air, simple, hospitable and, above all, peace-loving.
And as he got back in his car, the usually grim Premier
was beaming.

You couldn't help thinking that maybe, just maybe, a
little of the Spirit of Glassboro, New Jersey, had rubbed
off.

Relieve Stomach Distress

You keep reading about these "newly emerging nations"
in Africa and places like that. Personally, I'm all for them.
But every time I hear of another new nation bravely
emerging, this same nagging question runs through my
mind:

"Why?"

Maybe I wouldn't feel this way if I hadn't read *A Recent
History of the Republic of Mbonga and How It Emerged*.
Which I just wrote. It follows.

For centuries, the Secret Valley of Mbonga lay hidden

from the outside world. Its natives tended their flocks, tilled their vineyards and greeted each other daily with a gay smile and the single word, "mbonga." Which means, "Mind your own business."

Its discovery by a team of drunken spelunkers caused a worldwide sensation. Forty-two minutes later a long string of ambassadors from the leading powers crawled through the tunnel into the valley to present their credentials.

"Take us to your chief," said the Ambassadors of an elderly Mbongan who happened to be passing by.

"Chief?" said the startled Mbongan.

"You know, the head of your government."

"Government?" said the Mbongan.

"Good Lord!" said the Ambassadors and immediately called in a U.N. Truce Team to supervise the first free elections ever held in Mbonga. A ne'er-do-well Mbongan named Clauswitz was unanimously elected Chief. Primarily because he was the only native who bothered to vote.

"Congratulations," cried the Russian Ambassador. "Mbonga is now officially A Newly Emergent Democratic Republic Struggling To Throw Off the Yoke of Capitalist Imperialism. Allow us to send you ten billion rubles for your People's Army of Liberation."

"We don't have an army," said Chief Clauswitz.

"You will," said the Russian Ambassador.

"Congratulations," cried the American Ambassador. "Mbonga is now officially A Bastion of Democracy Struggling To Stem the Tide of Red Communism. Allow us to send you ten billion dollars to meet the wants of your people."

"We don't have any wants," said Chief Clauswitz.

"You will," said the American Ambassador. And to make sure he presented the Mbongans with twenty-seven television sets.

The Mbongans gathered around the television sets and tuned in the six o'clock news. It was all about stomach distress, the hydrogen bomb, headache miseries, an airplane crash, stomach distress, traffic fatalities, nasal congestion, race riots, and stomach distress. The Mbongans looked at each other and took up a collection to send Chief Clauswitz to the U.N. At the U.N., Chief Clauswitz took the rostrum, smiled gaily at the representatives of the other 111 nations, and delivered the briefest speech in U.N. history.

"Mbonga," he said.

He then went home, filled in the tunnel personally, and no Mbongan was ever seen again.

So hats off, I say, to Mbonga. It's the only newly emergent nation that's got a foreign policy I can understand.

An Alien Ideology

It was on May 24, 1982, that a flying saucer materialized before the General Assembly of the United Nations, hovered for a moment, deposited a scroll, hummed brightly, and vanished. The shocked delegates, who had been on the verge of a fistfight, stood frozen in awe as the Secretary General hesitantly picked up the scroll and read aloud its text:

"Human beings, listen and listen well. We are the Horruglies, a race of creatures who are seven feet tall, green-fanged and incredibly slithery. We have conquered half the galaxy and we will return in precisely ten years to accept your abject surrender."

"We shall never surrender!" cried the President of the United States.

"We shall never surrender!" cried the Premier of the Soviet Union.

"Mbunga!" cried the chief of the Ugulap Indians, meaning the same thing. And so agreed all the world's leaders.

Naturally, the President had to call off the war in Vietnam to conserve military strength. Naturally, the Soviet Premier had to make friends with the Chinese and Albanians to present a popular front. Naturally, the Chief of the Ugulaps gave up eating missionaries "to save room," as he put it bravely, "for the Horruglies." And General De Gaulle joined NATO, SEATO, the Warsaw Pact and the California Wine Promotion Board.

Not only were political and economic differences forgotten before the common threat of the Horruglies, but so were racial quarrels, too. True integration was achieved overnight, even in Alabama. "If it's seven feet tall, green-fanged and incredibly slithery," thundered the South's perennial presidential hopeful, "I ain't about to let it marry my sister."

For the first time, human beings were conscious that being human beings was far more important than being this or that. And so they worked together shoulder to shoulder in universal peace and the brotherhood of man. At precisely the appointed moment, the flying saucer materialized again in the U.N. Waiting to greet it were the world's leaders, linked arm in arm in brave defiance. A hatch slowly opened and out stepped two Horruglies—each being a furry-little, cuddly-little, bunny rabbit.

"But you're not seven feet tall, green-fanged and incredibly slithery!" cried the President.

"No," said the first bunny rabbit in some embarrassment, "we just said that to scare you. Honest, we wouldn't hurt a fly."

"You see," explained the other, "our only job is to give worlds what they want. And you've always wanted peace and brotherhood. Aren't you happy?"

The President turned to the Premier: "It's a rotten Commie plot." The Premier replied with a left to the brisket. Within an hour fourteen wars, seventeen revolutions and countless riots erupted. And the Ugulaps were fatter by two Baptists and an Episcopal Bishop.

"It's the first time we've failed," said one bunny rabbit sadly viewing the havoc.

"Well," said the other, "at least we found out what they wanted."

Part Four

IT, THE WAR

Uncle Sam Needs You

The Strange God Named Freedom

Once upon a time there was a land called Wog. It was a bountiful land with purple mountains and fruited plains. The people worshiped a deity called Freedom. Freedom was a generous god. He enriched the people's lives and blessed them with abundance. In gratitude the people would hold periodic rituals in his honor. Once each generation they would gather in the town square and beat drums and wave flags and blow bugles and say incantations. Then the very bravest, the very strongest, the very finest young men would step proudly forth. Oh, how the people admired them. Young girls would embrace them. Old men would shake their hands. For days they were feted and toasted and universally envied. Then their heads were chopped off. It was the highest honor any young man could aspire to. And afterward, each was always referred to reverently as one "who had sacrificed himself on the altar of Freedom."

In this way, the people felt they were appeasing their deity. And it seemed fair. For the cardinal tenet of their religion was that people should be free to do as they wished. And if the young men wished to get their heads chopped off, that was their inalienable right.

But times change. And one day, when they had beaten the drums and waved the flags and blown the bugles and said the incantations in the town square, not nearly enough brave, fine, strong young men stepped proudly forward.

"It isn't," said one, "that we don't believe in Freedom."

"It isn't," said another, "that we don't believe in sacrifices."

"It's mainly," explained a third, "that we just don't want to get our heads chopped off."

The leaders were aghast. "But Freedom demands sacrifices," they said, "namely you, you, you and you."

So the young men randomly selected were led off. And while young girls embraced them, it was woefully. And while old men shook their hands, it was sadly. And nobody envied them any more.

This made people uneasy. "It just doesn't seem fair somehow," they'd say. And when it was noted that rich young men were ducking, smart young men were hiding and the whole system was riddled with inequities, they demanded a change. The leaders, after thinking it over, came up with a wonderful idea. "We'll have a lottery," they said. "We'll draw names out of a hat. And every young man will have an absolutely fair and equal chance to sacrifice himself on the altar of Freedom."

This satisfied everybody. For now when a young man was led involuntarily away to have his head chopped off, he could no longer complain that it was because he was too poor or too stupid to escape that unwanted fate. No, it was merely a question of plain, dumb luck. And nothing, everybody agreed with relief, could be fairer than that.

Moral: Believe in Freedom, have a devout faith in fair play, and at all times carry a rabbit's foot.

Get in Step, Stupid

The following is another unpublished chapter in that standard unpublished reference work. *A History of the World, 1950–1999.* This chapter is entitled, "How War Became a Boon to Mankind."

The new trend was first noted in the 1960s with the deferment of college students who maintained high grades. This meant that to avoid the draft a young man had to be rich enough to attend college and smart enough to stay in. Consequently, the level of draftees grew steadily poorer and stupider. The catalyst that led to an even more enlightened draft policy was a statement by the Director of Selective Service, General Hershey. He announced that ten antiwar demonstrators were being immediately called up because it was his policy to "draft delinquents first."

The nation generally applauded. "If these delinquents

don't like the war," people said with great logic, "let's send them out there to fight it." Politicians agreed. "To fight for our nation on the battlefield is a sacred privilege," said the President. "And any malcontent who opens his yap is going to get it."

Most approving of all were the geneticists. "For thousands of years," explained the eminent Dr. Homer T. Pettibone, "we have been sending our bravest and strongest young men off to be killed in war. Usually before they can breed. At last we have it in our grasp to reverse this disastrous genetic policy."

The Administration, after careful reflection and an exhaustive study of the low voter registration among the poor, agreed. And Congress quickly passed what came to be known as "Hershey's Law." Initially, this provided that only jobless high-school dropouts with criminal records could serve in the Army. But with the progressive lowering of standards, the nation was at last able to clean out its jails, mental institutions and welfare rolls. Naturally, this army of poor, stupid misfits was constantly defeated. But following a dramatic appeal "to the better instincts of mankind," the President was able to secure the signatures of all other powers to the Geneva Protocols of 1984. These provided that no country would field a soldier with an I.Q. over 60 or without a congenital physical defect.

Wars spread, casualty lists grew and nations cheered.

True, Hershey's Law had some side effects. Gold Star Mothers took down their flags, not wishing it known they had raised a poor, stupid misfit. Young ladies declined invitations to U.S.O. dances. And few wrote letters to our boys at the front, few boys at the front being able to read.

Unhappily, some poor, stupid misfits survived the wars and returned home. But they all joined existing organizations of professional veterans and fitted in quite well. So everybody was most happy with the workings of Hershey's Law—everybody, that is, but the poor, stupid misfits. But as the President said in patriotic ceremonies every November 11:

"These brave boys can rest in peace, secure in the knowledge they have truly given their lives for the betterment of mankind."

How To Dodge the Draft

Once upon a time there was an honest young man named Hector L. Kingsley, who didn't wish to be drafted. "I am as patriotic as the next man," said Hector honestly, "but above all else, I simply do not want to go kill Vietnamese, Dominicans, Bolivians or whomever we're killing this week."

All his friends asked him, "Why not?" Hector mulled this question over a great deal. Finally he said honestly, "Well, I guess it's mainly because I don't know any Vietnamese, Dominicans, Bolivians or whomever. And it's very difficult to want to kill people you don't know."

His friends shook their heads and said he didn't understand American foreign policy. "I guess that's so," admitted

Hector honestly. "But I still don't want to kill people I don't know." And he resolved to do his utmost to dodge the draft.

At first he thought of becoming a conscientious objector. But he decided honestly that he wasn't that conscientious. Then he thought of applying for an exemption on the grounds his job was vital to national defense. But he had to concede honestly that jerking sodas wasn't that vital. He even considered marriage. But he finally told himself honestly he wasn't that desperate. Meanwhile, he grew thinner and paler and his friends worried about him. Several tried to explain American foreign policy to him. "We must contain Communism in Asia," they'd say. And Hector would nod honestly. "And we must prevent the spread of Communism in Latin America," they'd say. And Hector would nod honestly. "And therefore," they'd say, patting him on the back, "someone's got to go over there and kill people."

"People I don't even know?" Hector would ask. "I just can't bring myself to do it."

At last, a wise friend took Hector to a diplomatic reception. Now Hector, in addition to being honest and patriotic, also had a violent temper. And, fortunately, the Vietnamese Consul General accidentally spilled his vodka gimlet on Hector's best tie. Hector was furious. Then a Dominican general accidentally trod upon Hector's shiny black pumps. Hector was livid. Finally, a Bolivian or whomever, carelessly waving a cigar, burned a hole in Hector's trousers. The very next morning Hector appeared before his draft board to demand immediate induction.

The draft board, which consisted of an elderly lady, two retired pediatricians and a rising young attorney, were awfully glad to see a fine, honest, patriotic young man like Hector volunteering to do his part to keep America strong. They said he would make an excellent soldier.

"Yes," said Hector honestly. "For I hate Vietnamese, Dominicans, Bolivians or whomever. Give me a rifle, a bayonet and a napalm bomb. I want to shoot them in the head, stab them in the brisket and burn them to cinders. Kill! Kill! Kill!"

The members of the draft board looked at each other sadly, shook their heads and naturally rejected Hector as being mentally unstable.

Moral: It is perfectly all right to want to kill people. As long as you don't get emotionally involved.

The Man With the Crazy Idea

Once upon a time there was a man named Hirschel N. Rightly, forty-two, an electric-can-opener repairman of South Menachee, Wisconsin, who achieved a fleeting moment of fame.

The Nation was bogged down at the time in a vast war 10,000 miles away. It couldn't seem to win it, it couldn't seem to lose it, and it couldn't seem to get out of it. A bitter debate raged over this dilemma, with seemingly every conceivable view being aired. And then Mr. Rightly expressed an opinion about the war that absolutely no one had ever expressed before.

"I like it," he said.

Mr. Rightly casually expressed this opinion to a friend over beer and Polish sausages. The friend repeated it to the editor of the *South Menachee Weekly Clarion,* who wrote a little story. The wire services picked it up, and almost before Mr. Rightly knew it, he was appearing on that nationwide television program *Face the Press.*

"You like the war, Mr. Rightly?" asked a reporter. "I take it, then, that you're a Hawk."

"Oh, no," said Mr. Rightly. "The Hawks don't like the war at all. They want to win it and get it over with. The Doves, of course, just want to get it over with. And everybody else I talk to just wishes it would go away. Not me, though. I like it."

"Are you now or have you ever been . . ."

"A Communist? Gosh, no. I bet they want to get it over with too. They probably don't much like being bombed. But I'm dead against the Communist position on this one. In fact, I'm the only one I know who is."

"Why do you like the war, Mr. Rightly?"

"Well, it kind of makes the television programs more interesting. And there's some exciting new comic strips come out of it. Then I heard where it's a help to the economy. And after all, what would we talk about at parties and such? Without that war there'd be some mighty dull silences in the conversation."

"But with the President seeking peace . . ."

"Now don't you put me down as against the President. I think he's doing a fine job. From my point of view."

Despite probing questions, Mr. Rightly stuck to his guns: He liked the war. And he returned to South Menachee something of a celebrity. The following week his wife filed for a divorce.

"I can't stand people whispering all the time," she said. "You and your crazy ideas."

Sure enough, his friends began to avoid him as he insisted on expounding his view. He caught little phrases like "odd" and "some kind of nut." His employer fired him without giving a reason. Jobless, friendless and alone, he grew despondent and was at last committed to the state mental hospital. There, he sat staring at a wall and muttering:

"But if we send half a million men to war and then spend $30 billion a year on fighting it, someone must like it."

Then he would slap his forehead and add with a miserable groan: "But why did it have to be me?"

Moral: People get committed for crazy ideas; nations get committed to them.

The Only Fair Draft Law

It was on May 24, 1964, that Mildred Pettibone, Homemaker second class, greeted her husband, Homer, a Staff Sergeant at Macy's, with the news that their son had been drafted.

"There, there," said Homer, who had undergone a hard day in Women's Footwear. "I'm sure he'll be a credit to his uniform and his country."

"But he's only six weeks old," said Mildred with a frown.

Homer looked surprised. "Certainly you don't want to return to the old haphazard system of selective service." He shook his head. "No, it was perfectly clear all along that the only way to eliminate inequities was to draft everybody."

"I don't see why they couldn't still just draft all kids at eighteen for a couple of years and let it go at that," said Mildred.

"Now you know that didn't work," said Homer. "There were those kids, sweating it out in the Army or the Peace Corps or whatever. And there were we older people, sloshing down three-martini lunches and living it up in civilian life. Now, really, Mildred, you can't say that was fair."

"I still think I could have been a great actress," said Mildred with a toss of her head.

"Let's not get into that again," said Homer with a sigh as he took off his fatigue jacket with the Macy's Brigade shoulder patch. "They gave you the standard vocational tests when you were drafted and decided you could serve best as a Homemaker. You can't argue with the computers. And by the way, where'd you get that apron?"

"I found it in an old trunk," said Mildred, twirling around so that the organdy swirled. "Isn't it pretty?"

"It's non-reg. You know that if they catch you out of uniform once more, they'll bust you to Homemaker third class. Say! What rank did they give Homer Junior?"

"Apprentice Toddler."

"At six weeks? Not bad at all. Why, he could make First

Grader at five and get promoted to Teen-ager by eleven. Just think, Mildred, our boy may grow up to be Chief of Staff someday."

Mildred smiled at this evidence of fatherly pride. "Look," she said, lifting the child from his khaki-colored bassinet. "I've already sewn his chevron on his diaper."

"Oh, Mildred," cried Homer, "you really could be a first-class Homemaker if you tried. I'd be so proud of you. And with the extra pay and allotments, we could move to a better barracks."

Later that night, Mildred stood for a moment at the window in her khaki nightgown, looking at the moonlight. "You know," she said musingly, "sometimes I wish that instead of extending the draft they had simply abolished it. That would have eliminated the inequities, too."

Homer, shocked, sat bolt upright in his bunk. "Abolish the draft? What about our national security? Why, our enemies might have walked in and taken over."

He adjusted his regulation pajamas, settled back on his regulation pillow and pulled the regulation blanket up to his chin. "Good heavens, Mildred," he said, "how would you like to live in a totalitarian state?

Farewell to a Soldier

"Hey, I got my draft notice," he said with a tentative smile. "I go in two weeks."

I didn't know quite what to say. He's the son of a friend,

a big, handsome young man, intelligent, decent, polite. I've known him since he was twelve, not well, but enough to like him very much. And I didn't know what to say. You can't say, "Congratulations." After all, he wasn't volunteering to risk his life for some cause he believed in deeply. He was being drafted. He was being ordered to risk his life—to kill or be killed—or go to prison. You don't congratulate a friend who is given a choice like that. Nor can you say, "Oh, what a shame!" Not face to face, you can't. There he stood, so very young and alive. Perhaps he dreaded what lay ahead, but you could feel in him, too, excitement at the immediate prospect of leaving home, being on his own, manhood, adventure. And to say how awful you thought it was would be somehow betraying him.

So I didn't know what to say.

It was different, I think, in World War II. We had a cause then. One country, one cause. Bands and flags and U.S.O. girls. And when we young men signed up, they'd shake our hands and pat us on the back and tell us how proud of us they were.

"I wish I were twenty years younger," the old gaffers would say. "I'd sign up myself."

And maybe it was a lousy war, boring and bloody like all wars. But how bravely we marched off to it, excited and proud, confident of the righteousness of our cause, the phrases of gratitude and encouragement and envy ringing in our ears. But I couldn't even give this young man that. I couldn't tell him I envied him. I didn't. I couldn't tell him I was proud he was going. I wasn't. I couldn't tell him how righteous was his cause. I'm far from sure of that.

So I didn't know what to say.

"I think I'll get in the Marines maybe," he said with that tentative, almost-questioning smile.

I thought of how we'd gotten into this war. And how we'd let it grow over the years. And of how we couldn't seem to win it or lose it or end it. And because we couldn't find any way to win it or lose it or end it, we were now sending him out to fight it. To risk his life. To kill or be killed. What I wanted to say most was how terribly sorry I was. But you couldn't say that.

We talked for a few minutes about where he might be sent for training and what he would do when he got back. Then we shook hands, he still with that tentative smile, and I said, "Well, lots of luck," and he nodded and went away.

And so we sent still another young man off to fight still another war, the way nations have for centuries. And maybe I shouldn't have felt ashamed and inadequate. Yet how totally we've failed when we don't know what to say.

West Vhtnnng, a Brief History of

Ngone for Ngood

Don't ask me what's happening in South Vietnam. Last I heard our State Department's coup was being fiercely resisted by the C.I.A.-trained palace guard. And Madame Nhu was seeking political asylum in Disneyland. Besides, right now I'm very busy composing a new chapter of my *History of West Vhtnnng*. I know you'll be delighted to hear it has a happy ending.

You recall West Vhtnnng. It's that lovely, sleepy little Asian country where everybody loved everybody. Then one day, President Ngo Mahn Ngo got a bright idea. He dropped Washington a postcard. "Help!" he wrote. "I am a bastion of democracy under attack by the dread Viet-Narians. Who are all Moscow-trained peasants and would-be dictators. Send aid. No checks, please."

For years, things went swimmingly. The State Department sent Mr. Ngo $1.5 million a day. The C.I.A. sent him swarms of agents. And the Pentagon sent him 16,500 military advisers. Mr. Ngo was able to concentrate the peasants in barbed-wire camps (called "Sunset Happiness Homes"), educate the students in barbed-wire education centers (called "Re-education Centers") and build a huge Loyal Royal Army (called "The greatest force for nonviolence the world has ever seen").

And nobody complained. Not more than once, anyway.

As years went by, a terrible thing happened. Americans got the idea it wasn't a very hot democracy Mr. Ngo had there. In fact, they said, it was a lousy dictatorship. And, really, it was very immoral of us to support a lousy dictatorship. Something must be done.

And it was. Some credited the State Department. Some the C.I.A. But actually, it was the Pentagon, who by now had one U.S. military adviser in the field for every .8 Loyal Royal Army troop.

For years, the advisers had been advising the troops: "Men, let us march upon the enemy and save Vhtnng from tyranny!" And at last the message sank in! At last the Loyal Royal troops laid aside their shptunngs (a kind of one-stringed ukelele), picked up their rifles and marched! They marched straight up to the Presidential Palace and kicked out Mr. Ngo.

So everything ended happily.

The State Department was happy with the new military junta because it's very familiar in dealing with military juntas. The C.I.A. was happy because it kind of instinctively likes to overthrow governments. And the Pentagon was happy because it proved that we can get a backward, un-civilized people like the Vhtnnngians to go out and kill each other, given a proper incentive.

Best of all, Americans everywhere were happy because we finally tossed out that lousy old dictatorship. In favor of a brand new dictatorship. Which proves that morality will triumph in the end.

So we were able to get on with the war, now that everybody was happy. Except maybe the Vhtnnngian people. I don't know whether they were happy or not. I don't think anybody asked.

Leader of the Week

Let us pause to salute the leader of our loyal allies in South Vietnam. Whoever he may be today. For we have won another smashing victory. Not over the guerrillas, exactly. But over neutralism. This new general who overthrew the junta which deposed President Diem who succeeded Emperor Bao Dai says he is violently opposed to neutralism. Which, he says, is why he overthrew the junta. Which, the junta said, is why it overthrew Mr. Diem. And so on. Of course, this latest coup meant our military advisers had to cancel a major offensive scheduled for the very next morning. But that's the way it goes. Oddly enough, that's the way it went for years in the neighboring bastion of democracy called West Vhtnnng, the only Asian bastion I'm an expert on.

It was in the thirty-seventh year of our lightning campaign to wipe out the dread Viet-Narians, who were all Moscow-trained peasants. The benevolent leader of Vhtnnng at the time was General Hoo Dat, who had recently overthrown General Hoo Dar, successor of deposed General Hoo Nhows, who followed Daw Ghakt. And January was only half over. In Washington, our Secretary of Defense, gravely concerned, issued a clarifying statement. "The war is going amazingly well," he said proudly. "Except we are losing our shirts."

This alarmed our military advisers in the field, who immediately advised an all-out offensive, advising the Loyal Royal Army, as usual, "to fight to the death" for the beloved Vhtnnng. Or else. And this, as usual, panicked the Loyal Royal Army. An emergency meeting of the High Command is called. "Gentlemen," says General Hoo Nhows, "there is no question that if our ferocious Loyal Royal troops hone their bayonets, arm themselves to the teeth and hurl themselves upon the enemy, that awful catastrophe we have carefully avoided for thirty-seven years will occur: Somebody will get hurt."

There are gasps of horror from the assembled generals. "Maybe," says General Hoo Dar hesitantly, "it would be best to give up the long struggle and allow ourselves to be neutralized."

"What!" cries General Hoo Nhows. "And lose that $1 million a day in American aid? Why, the economy of our nation is at stake. Not to mention our villas on the Riviera. No, we have no choice. We must go through the usual routine."

"So soon?" complains General Hoo Dat. "It's not fair. I only got to be leader for three days."

"Let's not allow personal ambition to interfere with the good of our country," says General Hoo Nhows sternly. "All right, gentlemen. Draw straws."

So I'm convinced these constant coups by the Vietnamese generals against the Vietnamese general really are victories over neutralism. In a way. But I'm not at all sure neutralizing Vietnam's a bad idea. In fact, it gets more and more appealing. With each passing coup.

At the very least, I say, let us begin. Let us make a start in the right direction. For the sake of unity and clarity, let's neutralize the Vietnam Army.

If You Can't Lick 'Em

Our leaders in Washington are mulling over a brilliant new strategy: invade North Vietnam. And it certainly makes sense. If we can't win the war we're fighting in South Vietnam, I say, let's go fight it somewhere else. Oddly enough, I'm just the ace expert to inform everybody on this point. For I happen to be the only ace expert on the neighboring nation of West Vhtnnng. Where precisely the same question cropped up.

It was in the twenty-seventh year of our lightning campaign to wipe out the dread Marxist-Leninist Viet-Narian guerrillas. The Loyal Royal Army, under the command that week of General Hoo Dat Don Dar, burned as always with a spirit of fierce resistance. Primarily against the idea of fighting anybody. Our Secretary of Defense was making his monthly "crisis mission" to Vhtnnng and had just issued his assessment to the press: "There is no cause for alarm in the catastrophic situation because around the corner lies either victory or something else and I pledge to have our boys out of the trenches by Christmas. Christmas of 1993."

He was in a grim mood when he met with General Hoo Dat Dar to confer. "The fact is, the war is going badly and we must take some bold, dramatic step," said our Secretary. "Surrender?" suggested General Hoo Dat Dar hopefully. "Never!" said our Secretary firmly. "We cannot afford to lose West Vhtnnng. Not to mention California, Illinois and both Dakotas in the fall election. No, the fighting Loyal Royal Army must launch a do-or-die invasion of the impregnable stronghold of East Vhtnnng."

"What are you," inquired General Hoo Dat Don Dar politely, "some kind of nut?"

"The alternative, as I see it," said our Secretary imperturbably, "is to redouble our effort here in West Vhtnnng. Our 15,000 military advisers will drop twice as many napalm bombs. We'll make twice as many strafing runs. Bomb! Burn! Destroy! With luck, we'll blacken every square inch of West Vhtnnng. Blood will flow in . . ."

"Blood?" said General Hoo Dat Don Dar. And he fainted dead away.

When they revived him, he made a speech: "Mr. Secretary, after due deliberation I feel I speak for all the people of West Vhtnnng in beseeching your 15,000 military advisers to lead a glorious invasion of East Vhtnnng. Rest assured the fighting Loyal Royal Army will be behind them to the man. Somewhere."

So, as I say, I'm sure the majority of South Vietnamese would be delighted if we would carry the war to North Vietnam. Or anywhere else.

Delicate Crisis

A few people may have been a tiny bit confused by what's been going on in Vietnam lately. But at last the historic meaning of it all lies revealed. You'll recall this last crisis started when our staunch democratic ally, General Nguyen Khanh, decided to grab some more power and become the strong man of South Vietnam. Our State Department promptly issued a statement saying this was a great idea because a strong man would promote lasting "national unity" and thus save Southeast Asia. Two hours later, our new strong man was fleeing for the hills. His successor, Mr. Oanh, said the General was suffering from "mental illness." And also had a bad cold. And he wouldn't be back. We said he would too. At last, the General called a press conference to say he wasn't either crazy, but he didn't wish to resume the seat of power at the moment. And why not? Well, if I may delicately quote the press dispatches on this touchy subject: "Khanh said he was suffering from hemorrhoids." Which explains everything.

Now, we once faced precisely the same sort of crisis in the neighboring nation of West Vhtnnng. It was in the eighteenth year of our lightning campaign to wipe out the dread Viet-Narians. But the current President of the Week, General Hoo Dat Don Dar, wasn't doing too well at spreading democracy. Mainly because he invariably fainted at the sight of blood. So our State Department decided that only a stronger man could save democracy in Southeast Asia. And we sent our Ambassador around to interview General Kar Toom. "Allow me to feel your muscle," said our Ambassador. "Fine, fine. And are you fully committed to the spirit of democracy?"

"Bomb, shoot, burn, kill!" cried General Kar Toom happily.

"Marvelous," said our Ambassador. So we overthrew General Hoo Dat Don Dar and installed General Kar Toom. At first, all went well. But it began to be noticed that General Kar Toom squirmed this way and that at the conference table, which gave him a shifty look. He refused to attend all social events but stand-up cocktails parties, offending many. And when anyone sat in his presence he looked pained, thus giving rise to rumors he had ambitions to become a royal monarch.

"You are getting unpopular," said our Ambassador worriedly. "To show you are democratically one with your troops, you must go out there and inspect the front lines. Now, a rugged three-day tour over rough back-country roads by jeep . . ."

"Ai-yee!" said the General. "I quit."

Fortunately the day was saved, thanks to a speedy investigation by the C.I.A. and an emergency shipment of technical aid from Washington—a dramatic operation known to every schoolboy as "The Relief of Kar Toom."

So, as I say, the historic meaning of it all now stands revealed: At bottom, every strong man has his flaws.

Of course, I think we could look pretty silly ourselves in history if we lose all of Southeast Asia. Merely for the want of a good proctologist.

A Good Year

It's time for our annual year-end review of West Vhtnnng, the only Southeast Asian country which makes any sense. And I'm glad to report all our observers agree that 1965 was a banner year in our lightning campaign to wipe out the dread Viet-Narian guerrillas—the best in decades. For there was no question that our 113,000 military advisers out there had at long last managed to instill a true fighting spirit in the Loyal Royal Vhtnnng Army.

Who can forget, for example, the stirring charge down from the hills of the Third Division led by General Hoo Dat Opp Dar? Nor the glorious defense of the capital by General Hoo Dat Don Dar? That the former succeeded in overthrowing the latter in this, the thirty-seventh coup of the year, is now enshrined as a footnote in Vhtnnng history. It's no wonder that by November all our observers were predicting victory in 1965. "If," as they put it, "we can somehow channel the Loyal Royal Army's new fighting spirit toward the enemy."

Unfortunately, this was a year that ended on a sour note. Our Ambassador had stopped by the palace to drop off the $2 million we were giving daily to bolster the stable, 48-hour-old government of General Hoos Nu—not knowing General Hoos Nu had been overthrown that morning while brushing his teeth by General Hoos On Phirst.

"Hoos in?" our Ambassador inquired politely of the butler. "Hoos out," the butler replied. "Who's in, then?" sighed our Ambassador. "Hoos in," agreed the butler. "Who's Hoo?" said our Ambassador irritably. "Hoos on Phirst," said the butler. At which point, our Ambassador lost his temper and hit the butler with a bladder. The noise frightened General Hoos On Phirst, who fled to Dalat (a villa on the Riviera) taking his stable government and $47 million with him. A passing janitor, Yu Hoo, seized the throne, he being handiest.

"Congratulations," said our Ambassador, wiping his brow, "on your stable government. Here's $2 million."

"To call this palace a stable is an insult to my janitorial pride," said Yu Hoo, folding his arms with dignity. "I won't take a nickel of your lucre."

This unprecedented act of defiance toppled three Cabinet members in Washington and two generals in the Pentagon. The 14th and 47th Divisions of the Loyal Royal Army, shouting, "Yu Hoo forever!" began fighting fiercely for national dignity. They fought the 32d, 19th and 437th Divisions of the Loyal Royal Army, who were fighting fiercely for more American aid.

Fortunately, however, all our observers still predicted victory in 1965. Some predicted it for the Yu Hoo force, some for the pro-American aid forces. A few still actually foresaw victory over the dread Viet-Narian guerrillas. "If," as they put it, "we can somehow pacify the fighting Loyal Royal Army."

Sweet Revenge

We sure showed them. As you know, a company of Viet Cong guerrillas snuck up on one of our bases in South Vietnam and bombarded our military advisers with mortar shells. So to teach them a thing or two, Mr. Johnson dispatched three aircraft carriers to make the first of a series of all-out bombing attacks. On North Vietnam. Now this makes sense. Because, as our generals say, you've got to attack your enemy's source of supply. And, as usual, the 81mm. mortar shells used in the raid turned out to have been made in the United States. For the guerrillas, as usual, had captured them from our loyal allies, the South Vietnam Army. So you can see where bombing North Vietnam makes a great deal of sense under the circumstances. Because the obvious alternative, of course, was to bomb ourselves. Personally, however, I prefer the solution we worked out in that neighboring bastion of democracy, West Vhtnnng.

It was in the twenty-third year of our lightning campaign to wipe out the dread Viet-Narian guerrillas. We were giving $2 million a day worth of arms and ammunition to our Loyal Royal Vhtnnng troops. But the dread Viet-Narians were growing better equipped every week. By about

$14 million worth. Our generals were understandably frustrated. "Above all else, we must cut off their sources of supply," they cried. "Let's bomb Communist East Vhtnnng! Or maybe Red China?"

It was a grave choice and our President didn't want to do anything rash. So he sent his aide, Mr. George McBundy, out to investigate. "Good Heavens!" said Mr. McBundy. "The dread Viet-Narians are swiping their arms and ammunition from the Loyal Royal Vhtnnng troops!"

"Great," says the President. "We'll teach those Viet-Narians a lesson they'll never forget. We'll bomb the Loyal Royal Vhtnnng Army." But this plan was opposed by our Secretary of State on the grounds we would lose face throughout Southeast Asia. "Besides," he inquired, "who is supplying the Loyal Royal Vhtnnng Army?"

So, after further investigation, a new plan was drawn up to bomb the U. S. Ammunition Depot at Sagebrush, Nevada. But the President vetoed this because Sagebrush had gone heavily Democratic in the last election. He also rejected a second plan to attack the Morning Glory Munitions Works of Elmwood, New Jersey, as he felt this would destroy the confidence of the business community.

"But we must cut off the Viet-Narians' source of supply," our generals insisted. Public clamor mounted. At last, the President decided on drastic action. He converted the Morning Glory Munitions Works into a buggy-whip factory, declared Sagebrush a pocket of poverty and imposed a worldwide embargo on the shipment of arms to the Loyal Royal Vhtnnng Army. It worked like a charm. The loyal troops, who were always afraid some of the stuff might go off accidentally in transshipment, were happy. And, as history records, the dread Viet-Narians eventually were forced to surrender. Having run out of ammunition.

Allies Like Us

Good news. After ten years of fighting in Vietnam we have come up with a bold new strategy for victory. It was announced in a headline in the New York *Times: "U.S. Is Planning Drive to Win Backing of Vietnamese for War."*

The story from Saigon said that Mr. Carl T. Rowan, Director of the U. S. Information Agency, ordered an all-out educational campaign to convince the South Vietnamese people whom we are fighting for that this is a good thing. And I say it's not a moment too soon. Actually, we once launched a similar campaign in the neighboring kingdom of West Vhtnnng. And everyone agreed that it certainly did clear the air.

It was in the twenty-fourth year of our lightning campaign to wipe out the dread Viet-Narian guerrillas. From the capital of Sag On, U. S. Information Specialist Second Class Homer T. Pettibone was dispatched to win the backing of the Vhtnnngians for the war. As he approached the little village of Cao Dung, Pettibone spotted a beloved Vhtnnngian peasant tilling his rice paddy. "Congratulations, beloved Vhtnnngian peasant," cried Pettibone, "the Americans are here to save you!"

"Ai-yee!" cried the beloved peasant. And he dove head-first into a ditch.

"No, no," said Pettibone reassuringly. "I don't mean the Americans are right here in Cao Dung. I mean we have come across the sea to help you beloved Vhtnnngians fight to the death for your beloved country. Which was created by Subparagraph IV of the Multilateral Accords reached at the Geneva Convention of 1954."

"Thanks a lot," said the peasant, cautiously raising his head. "Our battle cry," continued Pettibone, "is 'Save the Freedom-Loving Vhtnnngians!' Our only goal is to help you preserve your free, democratic society under your beloved Premier, General Hoo Dat Don Dar, whom I know you would be happy to die for."

"Excuse me," said the peasant, "but I believe it's Tuesday. On Tuesdays we are happy to die for General Hoo Dat Opp Dar. Under the recent convertible coup agreement, General Hoo Dat Don Dar is Premier on Mondays, Wednesdays, and alternate Fridays, except during summer vacation, and so we don't die for him on . . ."

"To be sure," said Pettibone, a bit testily. "But rest assured the full might of America stands behind your free, democratic right to die for whomever you want to die for. Ah, here comes some of our might flying towards us now. Move over."

When the bombers had gone, Pettibone and the peasant climbed out of the ditch and surveyed the smoking ruins of Cao Dung. "It is allies like you," said the peasant, all choked up, "who make it easy to die for one's country."

But as I say, this campaign in Vhtnnng cleared the air.

For after conducting several thousand more similar interviews with beloved Vhtnnngian peasants, we adopted a clear-cut new battle cry: "Save the freedom-loving Vhtnnngians! Whether they like it or not!"

Love for Sale

General Ky, the firmly entrenched Premier of the stable government of South Vietnam (as this is written), has come up with a stimulating idea for winning the war out there: He wants to establish roving bordellos for our boys at the front. Kind of like mobile libraries.

"After battle," says the Premier happily, "the troops would be able to go to these places for a little rest and amusement." Which certainly would boost the old morale. Experts, however, see no chance General Ky's generous offer will be accepted. They note a similar suggestion was once made in the neighboring bastion of democracy of West Vhtnnng. The reaction was just what you might expect.

It was in the twenty-eighth year of our lightning campaign to wipe out the dread Viet-Narian guerrillas. Our Ambassador stopped off at the Loyal Royal Palace to pay our daily respects and our daily $2 million to the Premier of the Week, General Hoo Dat Don Dar. But all he found was a note on the door saying, "In case anybody wants to overthrow me, I'm across the street at the Busy Bee Girls & Refreshment Club—General Hoo." The Club presented a gay scene with a pack of cheery GIs engaged in their favorite pursuit: namely a bevy of giggling Vhtnnngian maidens. The Ambassador spotted General Hoo seated on a bar stool in the corner moodily sipping the native drink Kokah-Kolah.

"Ah," said the Ambassador, slapping the General on the back, "isn't it heartwarming to see the way our 10,000 friendly American soldiers fraternize with the indigenous native population on a people-to-people basis?"

"I haven't been able to get a date for two weeks," said the General glumly. "Did you bring the $2 million? It may cover my bar bill. Boy, since your 25,000 troops arrived, prices have sure gone up around here."

"I trust," said the Ambassador, frowning, "that you are not complaining about the way our 90,000 fun-loving troops pursue rest and amusement. After all, we have always considered you a loyal ally worth every nickel of your friendship."

"Oh, no!" cried General Hoo, ducking as a bottle sailed over his head. "I can't express my awe and admiration for the indomitable will to conquest of your 125,000 GIs. The way they charge down here each night all the way from the front line . . . But wouldn't it be easier if we brought the rest and amusement to them? In comfy trailers? Think of the saving in time and energy. Not to mention our bar mirrors. Think, at ten piasters each, of the profit. Think . . ."

The Ambassador was horrified. "You mean a crass, commercial operation? How little you know us Americans. Our 175,000 boys don't want to purchase the affections of your maidens. They wish to win their respect and love through manly vigor. Even if it costs them fifty dollars each in drinks. That's the American way."

"Boy," said General Hoo with a sigh, "you Americans sure are inscrutable."

"All you have to understand, dear friend," said the Ambassador proudly, throwing an arm around the General's shoulders, "is that we Americans believe above all else that you cannot buy real love or real friendship. Now, how do you want your $2 million today, in cash or a postal money order?"

Take a Buddhist to Lunch

It was in the forty-seventh year of our lightning campaign to wipe the dread Viet-Narian guerrillas out of West Vhtnnng, which was a devoutly religious country. Although we faced other handicaps, too.

The two main religions were Buddhism and Christianity. The Buddhists devoutly believed in moderation in all things, contemplating the navel and clobbering any Christian they could lay their hands on. The Christians, on the other hand, devoutly believed in loving their enemies, turning the other cheek and clobbering any Buddhist they could lay their hands on. This resulted in what is called "a religious schism." And while the fighting spirit of the once-gentle Vhtnnngians grew, few found the necessary time or enthusiasm to fight the Viet-Narian guerrillas. Mainly because the Viet-Narians weren't very religious. But just when all looked blackest, a new organization was formed—the National Council of Christians and Buddhists. Its leader was a humble Vhtnnngian peasant trained on Madison Avenue— Ba Nai Brith.

First, Ba Nai Brith went to the leader of the Buddhists, Trich (venerable) Oh Treet. "As a devoutly religious leader," he said, "you should act civilized and practice human brotherhood above all." Trich Oh Treet contemplated his prayer wheel, a photograph of Alan Watts and several navels. "You are right," he said with a sigh. "We must remember that goodness, kindness and brotherhood with all living things are the path to Nirvana." Ba Nai Brith then went to the leader of the Christians, General Krish Mah Phut, who contemplated an old rosary, a photograph of Douglas MacArthur and the numerical inferiority of his followers. "You are right," he said with a sigh. "We must remember that goodness, kindness and brotherhood with all living things are the path to Heaven."

Oh, what a glorious day it was! Premier Hoo Dat Don Dar himself signed the proclamation declaring National Brotherhood Week. The prettiest girl in Vhtnnng, How Bot That (47"–24"–26"), was named "Miss Anti-Defamation League." A Christian family moved into an all-Buddhist neighborhood and two Buddhist boys attended a Christian school without being spat upon.

"At last we have become a modern, civilized nation practicing true human brotherhood," said Ba Nai Brith in a statment to the press.

And to prove the success of the week he released figures showing that the Vhtnnngian Buddhists and Christians, having laid aside their differences, killed a record 2347½ Viet-Narian guerrillas. By actual body count.

"Victory is just around the corner," said the U. S. Defense Secretary happily. "Again."

But as in every civilized country, the moment Brotherhood Week ended, the Christians and Buddhists returned to their devotions—clobbering each other right and left. And the war dragged on.

"It's a shame," said the Defense Secretary sadly, "that these people can't celebrate Brotherhood Week the year round."

A Flat-out War

It was in the thirty-eighth year of our lightning campaign to wipe the dread Viet-Narian guerrillas out of West Vhtnnng when a dispute arose on how best to save that beleagured nation for democracy. Some strategists favored bulldozing a 200-yard wide "Death Strip" between West Vhtnnng and East Vhtnnng. And some strategists favored declaring the entire border province of Whar Dat a "Free Kill Area" in which anything that moved would be blasted. It was the U. S. Military Commander, General Zipp K. Zapp, whose clear thinking resolved the issue. "Both plans have merit in our unending struggle to save our beloved allies," he said thoughtfully. "So let's stop talking and start doing."

"Do which, sir?" said an aide.

"Do both, damn it," said General Zapp.

And so it was that the entire province of Whar Dat was bulldozed flat and declared a "Free Kill Death Strip Hands Up Don't Move Democracy Loving Area."

Naturally, such an ambitious undertaking was not accomplished without some carping. Indeed, the Provincial Governor of What Dat, General Ngo Mahn Ngo, dictated an eloquent letter of protest to his Premier, General Hoo Dat Don Dar. Unfortunately, the letter was never transcribed, as Governor Ngo succumbed to an uncontrollable urge to scratch his left ear while seeking a phrase. This drew and immediate response from forty-two Strategic Air Command bombers. And Ngo Mahn Nago was ngone. This ended the protest movement in Whar Dat. In fact, it ended all movement.

"I am proud to report that the province of Whar Dat, for the first time in thirty-eight years is entirely free of Viet-Narian guerrillas and thus secure for democracy," General Zapp reported proudly to the President. "Please color it red, white and blue on your map."

"I think you've found a way out of this scrape we're in," said the President jubilantly. "Keep scraping."

Thus it was that the bulldozers ground forward to the next province, Opp Krik, and scraped that clean, too. Victoriously moving on, they had flattened half of West Vhtnnng by the next January. Everyone was delighted with the new strategy.

"This is getting to be the cleanest war we ever fought," the Army said happily.

"Our pilots have not mistakenly bombed a friendly village in months," the Air Force said happily.

The only person who wasn't absolutely delighted was Premier Hoo Dat Don Dar. "I'm not complaining, mind you," he said, "but the Loyal Royal Palace is sure getting filled up with my poor relations from what used to be the sticks."

He said that just before the bulldozers smashed through the East Portico.

And so it was that peace and total victory came at last to West Vhtnnng. Our President himself in a broadcast to the surviving Vhtnnngian people summed it all up.

"We have honored our commitment to stem the tide of Communism in Asia," he said, "and make your beloved Vhtnnng safe for democracy."

There was no question that the President's stirring words would have met with heartfelt applause from the grateful survivors. But none of the seven wanted to make the first move.

General Zapp Ends the War

It was in the forty-fifth year of our lightning campaign to wipe the dread Viet-Narian guerrillas out of West Vhtnnng. And even our Loyal Royal allies were getting a little tired of the whole thing.

"I have a new strategic plan that is bound to bring peace to West Vhtnnng," the Premier of the Week, General Hoo

Dat Don Dar, confided to the head of the American troops, General Zapp. "Why don't you go invade East Vhtnnng?"

"Marvelous idea," said General Zapp. "If you can't lick 'em, I always say, go lick somebody else."

So General Zapp led his army out of the tired old jungles of West Vhtnnng and into the fresh new jungles of East Vhtnnng. Naturally, there was some protest in the United States, based mainly on the fact that America wasn't at war with East Vhtnnng. But as the President said: "East Vhtnnng has been supplying the guerrillas of West Vhtnnng with arms, pickled rice and chicken soup. We must interdict these supply lines and destroy the forces of aggression at their source." And that certainly made sense. After a couple of years' fighting in East Vhtnnng, General Zapp didn't seem to be getting anywhere. Of course, it was much quieter in West Vhtnnng. Except that the distant artillery sometimes disturbed General Hoo Dat Don Dar's sleep.

"I have a new strategic plan that is bound to bring peace to both East and West Vhtnnng," he wired General Zapp. "Why don't you go invade Red China? Everybody knows they've been supplying the East Vhtnnngians with arms, peanut brittle and cherries jubilee."

"Marvelous idea," cried General Zapp. And he led his army out of the jungles of East Vhtnnng into Red China.

This caused some protest over getting involved in a land war in Asia. But that issue resolved itself when General Zapp discovered the Chinese were being supplied with arms, scones and gooseberry jam by the Russians. His army's long march across the Gobi Desert and its attack on Moscow are a matter of military history.

Indeed, Moscow might have fallen had not General Zapp captured documents proving the West Germans had been selling arms, rutabagas and chocolate sauce to the Russians for years.

"We must stop the forces of aggression at their source," cried General Zapp out of habit as his troops marched into Bonn. "Find out who's been supplying these Germans!"

Well, that, of course, was the turning point. Space forbids recounting General Zapp's further adventures. Suffice it to say his siege of Washington will long live in American military annals. Back in West Vhtnnng, whose name nobody could remember any more, a statue of General Zapp was erected by the natives in the now-sleepy village square. The simple inscription said:

"To General Zapp, who marched off to give us peace. In gratitude from a grateful West Vhtnnng, which was behind him all the way."

The Treaty of West Vhtnnng

It was in the forty-ninth year of our lightning campaign to wipe the dread Viet-Narian guerrillas out of West Vhtnnng that the miracle occurred: By bombings, cajolery and the greatest peace offensive the world had ever seen, our President was at last able to force the Communists to the bargaining table! And after months of haggling, the representatives of Hanoi, Peking and the U.S. were finally able to reach an agreement: A coalition government would be set up in West Vhtnnng pending free elections.

"It isn't perfect, sir," the weary U.S. negotiator reported to the President. "But it's the best we could hope for."

"Thank God, peace at last!" said the President with a sigh. "Have our Ambassador to West Vhtnnng tell the good news to our brave and loyal ally, Premier . . . Premier Whatshisname."

And so it was that the Ambassador burst into the Loyal Royal Palace. "Huzzah!" he cried, clapping the Premier on the back and doing a little jig. "Peace at last!"

The Premier, whose name, of course, was General Hoo Dat Don Dar, examined his fingernails and replied: "Says who?"

"Says who?" said the Ambassador, incredulously. "Why Hanoi, Peking, and America have all signed this seventy-two-page treaty guaranteeing that you and your Viet-Narian compatriots will lay down your arms and walk together into the golden sunset hand in hand."

"With those dirty rats?" said General Hoo. "Not on your life. They'd kick me out of my Loyal Royal Palace, strip me of my dancing girls and chop off both my gold-fringed epaulets. Not to mention what lies in between. No sir, I shall fight on to the last Loyal Royal soldier. Total victory shall be ours!"

"Says who?" said the Ambassador irritably.

"Says Hoo!" said the General adamantly, folding his arms and sticking out his lower lip.

At the very same time, Communist Premier Ho Ho Ho was breaking the good news of the peace treaty to the leader of the dread Viet-Narian guerrillas, whose name no one could ever remember.

"With those dirty rats?" cried the leader of the dread Viet-Narians. "Not on your life. They'd double-cross us again and swipe all the taxes we've squeezed out of the peasants. No sir, I shall fight on to the last guerrilla. Total victory shall be ours!"

America had to admit that it was, after all, the Viet-Narians' war for national liberation. So the war for democracy and national liberation continued to drag on.

But, actually, everything worked out very well. Our President was so mad at General Hoo's ingratitude that we withdrew all 750,000 American military advisers and cut off all economic aid. Premier Ho was so mad that he did likewise to the Viet-Narians. Deprived of napalm, bombers and automatic weapons, the two backward, uncivilized little armies in the backward, uncivilized little country could manage to kill only a couple of Vhtnnngians a week. The way they used to. So the Vhtnnngians were much happier.

As for the Communist bloc and the Free World, they soon found a nice, flat country without a lot of jungles and swamps where they could fight a big, modern, civilized war. So they were much happier, too.

Victory

It was a glorious sight. The flags of the United States and West Vhtnnng flew bravely side by side over the ros-

trum. Excitement flowed through the capital of Sag On. For
at long last the war to save this Southeast Asian nation from
Communism had been won.

"It is with a tremendous sense of accomplishment," said
the U. S. Secretary of Defense, "that we gather here to
celebrate V-V Day. There were some faint hearts who said
we could never wipe out the dread Viet-Narian guerrillas.
But we pledged to save our beloved friends, the Vhtnnngians, if it took us a hundred years. And we have not
only done so, my friends, but we have done so thirteen years
ahead of schedule.

"Here with us today to share equally in our hour of
triumph is the entire surviving population of West Vhtnnng.
His name is—let's see—Mr. Thang Sa Lot. Would you care
to say a few words on this historic occasion, Mr. Thang?"

An incredibly elderly gentleman in peasant pajamas and
coolie hat shuffled to the microphone, clasped his hands,
bowed and said: "I wish to thank the mighty United States
Government for saving me from Communism."

With that he sat down. The Secretary looked somewhat
miffed. "Really, Mr. Thang," he said, "I feel you might say
a little more than just that. After all, as a representative
of our brave allies, the freedom-loving Vhtnnngian peoples,
you . . ."

"Excuse me," said Mr. Thang, "*I* am the freedom-loving
Vhtnnngian peoples."

"True," said the Secretary. "And I'm sure you, the
Vhtnnngian peoples, appreciate the fact that to insure your
democratic processes three generations of American troops

have been bombing, blasting and fighting night and day from one end of your lovely little country to the other."

"Ah," said Mr. Thang with a nostalgic sigh. "My lovely country. When I was a boy . . ."

"Now look here, Thang," said the Secretary, frowning, "I don't want to accuse you of ingratitude. But to preserve your freedom we've gone through $212.3 billion, 123,748 tons of bombs and 93 stable Vhtnnngian governments. Even now as we look up, the sky is filled with those who did so much to save you Vhtnnngian peoples—American pilots in Americans planes which . . ."

"Ai-yee!" cried Mr. Thang, falling flat on his face. "Take cover!"

"It's only a fly-over to honor our mutual victory," said the Secretary irritably. "Please pick yourself up. Remember, you are a living example to all other Southeast Asian nations that they can count on their ally, America, to fight to the last to save them from Communism."

"The only living example," said Mr. Thang, nodding.

"After all," said the Secretary, putting his arm around him, "that's what this war was all about—setting a good example. And surely, you who have been through it must have some ringing message for your neighboring nations who face the same menace."

Mr. Thang surveyed the smoking countryside, thought for a moment and at last spoke up. "With America as an ally," he said, "who fears Communism?"

The War for Real

Making Progress

"Follow me, lad," cried the Kindly Old Philosopher, waving a somewhat rusted cavalry saber around his kindly old head. "I'm off to sack Hanoi. Oh, there's maidens and booty to be had for the taking."

Booty?

"Right, lad," he said, fire in his kindly old eye. "For some reason, our brave American boys ain't rushing down to sign up for the colors. And I aim to give them something to fight for. Oh, we'll pillage and burn and loot and we'll all come home rich and famous."

Wait a minute, I said. Thanks to the progress of civilization no one's fought a war for booty for hundreds of years.

"That's progress?" he said. "Well, then, how about Manifest Destiny? Rally 'round the flag, boys. Westward the course of empire. Today America, tomorrow the world!"

I explained he was still behind the times. We have clearly renounced any territorial ambitions in Asia. After all, nations have progressed beyond simple wars of conquest.

"That's progress?" he said. "Well would you believe the White Man's Burden?"

I shook my head.

"Hmmm," he said thoughtfully. "Then we'll have to fan the flames of patriotism. We'll sing war songs: 'Over there, over there . . .' Young gals will hand out the white feathers of cowardice on the street to young lads not in uniform. And our brave doughboys, with smiles on their lips, will march off to defend our sacred hearths from the barbarous gooks, who . . ."

Gooks?

"Like the bloody Huns and the treacherous Nips before them. We've got to have a dirty name for all these cruel and crafty Vietnamese people we hate."

But half of them were loyal, decent and freedom-loving —the half on our side.

"Then we'll need a ringing battle cry, like, 'Remember . . .' Hold on. Where was it these sneaky North Vietnamese launched their sneaky bombing attack on us which started the whole shebang?"

Well, I said, it was kind of the other way around.

"But," he said, scratching his head with the hilt of his saber, "if we ain't fighting for booty, conquest, patriotism or revenge, what the hell *are* we fighting for?"

Basically, I explained, we were attempting to check the growing Communist Chinese sphere of influence in South-

east Asia. For under the Domino Theory, it becomes geo-
politically necessary to . . .

"That's progress?" he said. "Well, it don't fire up my
blood none."

Nor anybody else's either, I said. The Doves want to
end it by negotiations, the Hawks want to end it by more
bombing, and everybody else just wishes it would go away.

"You mean we're finally fighting a war that nobody likes?"
The Kindly Old Philosopher sheathed his saber and smiled
reflectively. "You know, son, I think you're right. That's
progress."

Fatten Them Up

I'm glad to see where all the ace experts finally agree
on how come we're losing that war in Vietnam: It's too small.

Naturally, this is terribly frustrating. To examine the
problem in depth and explore possible solutions, I called in
my military affairs analyst, Corporal Homer T. Pettibone,
U. S. Army Flying Corps (retired).

Q—Corporal, is it really true we're losing in Vietnam
because the war is too small?

A—Yes, quite so. The Viet Cong enemy now number
only some 25,000 regulars. We have, as you know, some
22,000 U.S. military advisers in the field, plus more than
100,000 loyal Vietnamese fighting men. Who are mostly
fighting loyally among themselves.

Q—But with five-to-one odds on our side . . .

A—Oh, yes, we should be able to lick the Viet Cong with one arm tied behind our backs. After all, we have the most modern fighting force the world has ever seen. Take anti-tank warfare. Our best military minds, as the result of a twelve-year study, have at last devised computer-oriented antitank tactics which guarantee a 97.2 percent chance of victory against tanks no matter what their deployment. But in Vietnam we faced an unexpected problem.

Q—The problem is terrain?

A—No, the problem is the Viet Cong don't have any tanks.

Q—I see.

A—Similarly, our advanced work at the War College in massed artillery barrages, armored division maneuvers and nuclear-missile deployment has all gone for naught in Vietnam.

Q—A shame. What can be done to crush the Viet Cong?

A—Obviously, we have no choice. We must launch an all-out recruitment drive and send every available tank, gun and plane to Vietnam.

Q—To our American boys in the trenches out there?

A—No, no. To the Viet Cong.

Q—You mean we ought to recruit more enemy soldiers and give them better weapons?

A—Yes, of course. Once the enemy has a good-sized, well-equipped, modern army, we will regain the advantage our superior military skill gives us. We'll smash them in three months!

Q—But . . .

A—Ah, to wage a decent, full-scale war once again. Ah,

the battlefield maneuvers, the aerial dogfights, the intriguing challenges of strategy and tactics.

Q—But . . .

A—Oh, I can't describe the bitterness and frustration our keenly trained military leaders have undergone the past fifteen years. First Korea, now this. As General Sherman said: "Limited war is hell!" But now, with this new plan . . .

Q—But, Corporal, the public will never approve sending tanks and guns to the enemy.

A—Damn civilians! Always dragging their feet.

Q—I understand the problem, Corporal. But, really, there must be some other way to overcome the handicap of this being too small a war.

A—Have faith in the military, son. We'll think of something.

Commies Are Inhuman

Well, there goes the old Vietnam War. The fiendishly clever Communist guerrillas have outfoxed us. They've found a sure-fire way of sneaking their supplies into South Vietnam. And we can't lay a glove on them. As you know, they used to pack the supplies down the Ho Chi Minh Trail on their backs. And our pilots would bomb and strafe the bejeepers out of them. But now these guerrillas have come up with a defense we can never crack: elephants.

This disturbing news was revealed by a U.S. military spokesman in Saigon. He said our observation planes have already spotted two herds of pack elephants along the Ho

Chi Minh Trail. And, obviously, it won't be long until the guerrillas' entire supply system is elephantized. You can see the incredible brilliance of this Communist strategy. We can bomb villages and strafe rice paddies. And if some women and children and peasants get killed, it's a shame. That's war. But I ask you, what decent American could bring himself, no matter what the circumstances, to bomb an elephant?

Oh, I know our pilots will give it the old college try. You can envision Major Buck Ace of Centerville, U.S.A., at the controls of his attack bomber. He spots a suspicious movement along the trail below. He peels off on his strafing run. And there in his sights looms an elephant. An elephant! A big, gray, lumbering, gentle, lovable, old elephant. With huge, floppy old ears, a softly waving old trunk and sad, kindly old eyes.

What could more invoke the memories of childhood? Your first circus with the smells of hay, peanuts and canvas. Those Saturday movie matinees with Sabu and his beloved elephant friends. And Tarzan! Tarzan and his faithful Tembo, forever battling evil and sinister ivory hunters—evil and sinister because they want to slaughter elephants. Elephants! The very symbol of goodness, decency, friendship and gentle strength.

No, have no fear. The Major's eyes will mist up. His trembling hand will freeze on the trigger. And off he will zoom to bomb some village as the sly guerrilla mahouts chuckle among themselves and prod their beasts on down the trail in perfect safety.

True, our psychologists will struggle desperately to reorient our pilots, elephantwise. "You must think of these beasts," they will say, "as Communist-trained, Marxist-Leninist, Red elephants." And perhaps some calloused airman will actually manage to blow up an elephant. Before cracking up. But think of the reaction in this country! The public may solidly support bombing peasants. But elephants? Never. The S.P.C.A. would be up in arms. School children would be in tears. Liberals would unite. And though Republicans may currently favor escalating the war, they'll never condone potting the elephant.

And even if, by some wild chance, we talked ourselves into the proper anti-elephant spirit, that's only the beginning. For next the ruthless Commies will be hauling supplies by dog team—all the dogs being big, well-curried, gentle-eyed collies named "Lassie."

So there's no hope. The Communists have found our fatal weakness: We're just a nation of big-hearted old softies. When it comes to animals.

A White Paper

Herewith is another chapter in that hitherto unpublished textbook: *A History of the World 1950–1999*.

By the last half of the twentieth century, American diplomacy had made remarkable strides since the first crude days of the Republic when President Jefferson, wishing to negotiate with a foreign head of state, simply took pen in hand and wrote him a letter.

For example, in April of 1965 President Johnson decided

the time was ripe to offer "unconditional negotiations" with the Communists to end the war in Vietnam. Naturally, Mr. Johnson did nothing so unsophisticated as to write the North Vietnamese Government a letter. Instead, in keeping with modern diplomacy, he traveled to Baltimore, Maryland, and, in a major address, made the offer to the good people of Baltimore—the offer, that is, to negotiate unconditionally with the North Vietnamese. While a nervous world waited for the reaction, Tass, the Russian news agency, transmitted the offer from Baltimore to Moscow. There, a Chinese News Agency reporter lifted it from *Pravda* and sent it to Peking, where Radio Peking eventually relayed it to Hanoi. North Vietnamese Premier Pham Van Dong read of the offer in the Hanoi *Weekly Eagle* the following Tuesday over tea. Spluttering, he dashed off an angry letter to the editor declaring the whole thing "an unconditional insult."

On publication of the letter a week later in the *Eagle*, a subscriber mentioned it on a postcard to a cousin in Canton who was interviewed that day on a peasant-in-the-street broadcast over Radio Peking monitored in Yokohama by a bilingual ham operator whose brother-in-law sharpened bamboo brushes for the Tokyo *Illustrated Express*, which gave the story back-page headlines spotted by an alert American consulate employee while unwrapping fish.

The English translation of the Japanese story of the Chinese broadcast of the Vietnamese postcard of the Hanoi letter was promptly dispatched to Washington, where the National Security Council, after an exhaustive study of the text, said it was an offer of "unconditional surrender."

The President, delighted, agreed to send Premier Van Dong $2 billion "to rebuild his shattered nation." And, in keeping with modern diplomacy, he announced this generous offer to seven Boy Scouts who happened to be passing the White House on a guided tour. Unfortunately, due to one of the Scouts having a speech defect, the Tass reporter being drunk, a typographical error in *Pravda*, static in Peking and a hungover copyeditor in Hanoi, the headline in that week's *Eagle* read: "AMERICANS LAUNCHING TWO BILLION BOMBS."

Russia readied all her nuclear missiles. Peking launched a giant Chinese firecracker in a sampan aimed at Pismo Beach. The world was poised on the brink. The President, in desperation, picked up a pen and dashed off a letter, airmail, special delivery, to all heads of state, saying: "For heaven's sakes, let's not get panicky."

That did the trick and an uneasy peace once again reigned. But, as one State Department official sadly put it: "I fear this blunt action by the President has set American diplomacy back one hundred and fifty years."

The Russians Come to Grief

It was in late July that the South seceded again. The President said, "A house divided cannot stand!" Most Northerners nodded in agreement and said, "That's certainly true; thank goodness we're rid of it at last."

At first, North and South lived in peace. There was

even some talk about reunification through free elections. But the South's Premier, Colonel Jefferson Lee Stonewall, was not about to give the vote to Republicans, Negroes, Southern Liberals and other malcontents. Eventually, of course, these diverse groups united, revolted and launched a campaign of guerrilla warfare, espousing the doctrines of Abraham Lincoln and the tactics of General Sherman. Premier Stonewall countered with even greater repressions, such as herding all tenant farmers into "Strategic Hamlets." But these measures merely increased local sympathy for the guerrillas and they continued to gain ground.

The hopes of the North naturally lay with the guerrillas. But it refrained from formally sending troops on the grounds that it didn't want to go through the long and bloody Civil War all over again. And it contented itself with giving what covert aid it could. Northern clergymen, Negroes and Liberals slipped across the Mason-Dixon Line along the L.B.J. Trail, carrying pamphlets, brochures and other propaganda. Southern guerrillas were secretly trained at West Point, and the Northern press whooped it up for every guerrilla advance. Finally, in desperation, Premier Stonewall announced he was a Communist.

Actually, it was clear that no man could have despised the doctrines of communism more. But the Premier realized he could never shore up his tottering regime without outside help and he appealed to the Russians for aid. The Russian strategists promptly evolved "The Ptoshkin Theory," based on the Russian version of dominoes. "As the South goes," they said, "so goes Cuba, Guinea and Western Lithuania." And they began pouring two million rubles a

day and thousands of military advisers into the South to preserve "this bastion of socialism." Yet still the guerrillas
gained.

In frustration, the Russians at last issued a "Red Paper,"
which proved that 3.2 percent of the guerrillas come from
the North and 7.6 percent of their brochures were printed
in Saulk Center, Iowa. With this as an excuse, the Russians began bombing Northern border states, landed marines at Biloxi and conducted a naval bombardment of Coney
Island—all in an attempt to force the North to negotiate.
The North was outraged. Faceless hordes of Northern and
Canadian "volunteers" poured across the Mason-Dixon Line.
The Russians, in no position to fight a land war in such a
vast and distant country, were driven out and the nation was
reunified under the Northern Democrats.

It was the worst defeat ever suffered by World Communism. The loss in men, money and prestige was incalculable.
To this day, historians are divided on why Russia should
have been drawn into the wrong war for the wrong allies in
the wrong place at the wrong time. Some blame the Russians'
blind faith in their own invincibility. Others, sheer stupidity.

Battle Casualty

It is late in the winter of 1967. A blue-gray haze lies
outside my window. Last week they were talking about
peace in Vietnam. This week they are talking about "escalation" and "determination."

We are prepared, our leaders say, to go on fighting for years—years more. In the paper this morning there is a photograph of an American soldier hitting a Viet Cong prisoner with his fist. The caption begins by talking of the strains and frustrations of war. Then it tells how a company of American GIs caught three of the enemy hiding in a stream. In the photograph, the American soldier, knee-deep in the water, has just thrown a roundhouse right. His arm is still extended, fist clenched. He looks tall with close-cropped hair. He looks like any American.

The Viet Cong prisoner seems very small. He is naked from the waist up. His head has snapped back. His eyes are closed. His empty hands are raised before his face, palms inward, in a gesture that seems almost beseeching. It is not an unusual picture. That's the way war is. We have seen such pictures for years now.

I thought for a moment of how that American soldier must have felt. The frustrations and strains, I believed that. The fear during the hunt. The triumph of the capture. The anger at the whole bloody mess. The deep sense of satisfaction when fist slammed into cheek. Then, afterward, the rationalizations to wash away the guilt. I don't believe you can strike a smaller, unarmed, helpless man without feeling guilt—not the first time.

To do so, I believe, you have to close off a small corner of your mind, you have to callous over a small corner of your soul. You have to do this in the same way a fisherman does the first time he impales a living worm on a hook, the way a slaughterer does the first time he swings the sledge, the way a Nazi must have the first time he incinerated a Jew.

The first time is hard. But each time the callus grows. Each time is easier than the last. Eventually the time comes that you can do these things with neither sensitivity nor compunction.

Suddenly I felt sorry, not so much for the little Viet Cong, as for the big American soldier. I felt that what he did was understandable and human. Yet how sad it is to have a callus on your soul. How much less a living man it makes you. And how fast, in war, it grows.

And then I turned the page. For after all, we have seen such photographs for years now.

Later, thinking back on that photograph in this winter of 1967, I never felt more strongly that we must end this war in Vietnam. We must end the frustrations and strains and fears and triumphs and anger and satisfactions and guilt.

We must end it, not so much for their sake, as for our own.

A Scale of Values

The International Commission to Determine Human Worth has met in Geneva to set the relative value of American and Vietnamese lives. The meeting was called after charges were made in the U.S. that restrictions on bombing North Vietnamese civilians were endangering the lives of American pilots. "A single American boy," said one typical angry letter writer, "is worth a score of unfortunate Asians."

The American position was ably defended by the Honorable Homer T. Pettibone of the U. S. Bureau of Moral Weights and Measures.

"We do not contend, gentlemen," he began gravely, "that one American is worth a million Asians. Our restraint in using our nuclear weapons proves this. On the other hand, it would be a travesty of logic to argue that an American and a Vietnamese are of equal value. To begin with, Vietnamese are smaller. On a straight per-pound basis, they are obviously worth less. In addition, the average peasant neither dresses properly nor does he speak English, so that you must shout at him to penetrate his stupidity."

"Hear, hear," said the British delegate. "We felt the same about our Fuzzy-Wuzzies. Dashed good fighting men, though."

"True," said Mr. Pettibone, turning the point to his advantage. "But that, of course, is because he places such a low value on his own life. For example, we compensate the beneficiaries of friendly civilians we accidentally kill with a few hundred dollars. If they were Americans, each would cost us thousands. Now, while many of these peasants own their homes, few own their own cars, television sets or freezers. Clearly, they would be considered poor credit risks anywhere, simply because they aren't worth much."

"What non-Frenchman is?" said the French delegate with a shrug.

"Generally speaking," continued Mr. Pettibone, "they are poorly educated, ill-housed and underfed. Few read good books, play golf or even go to the movies. In a word, gentlemen, they are natives."

"Oh, natives," said the Belgian delegate, nodding. "We had to deal with them in the Congo and we know what they're worth."

"All we ask," said Mr. Pettibone, "is that this Commission set a fair ratio—say, thirty to one—so that we may go on bombing in good conscience."

A lively debate followed, highlighted by an hour-long speech by the German delegate on genetics, Nietzsche and the superiority of the Aryan race. In the end, a compromise of 28.2 Vietnamese per American was unanimously adopted.

"I feel this standard," Mr. Pettibone told reporters waiting outside, "accurately reflects the view of civilized people everywhere."

An irate African journalist protested that the Commission's members included only delegates from technologically advanced, Caucasian, Christian nations.

"Good heavens, man," said Mr. Pettibone in surprise, "who else is civilized enough to compare the value of human beings?"

The Great Debate Is Everywhere

"We have our commitments in Vietnam and we must honor them," said the Hawk, slapping his palm on the table for emphasis. "It's as simple as that."

"But what about the danger of escalation?" asked the Dove mildly. "Don't you worry about that?"

"It won't happen," said the Hawk firmly. "They don't want to get involved in a vast land war in Asia any more than we do. All we have to do is meet every aggressive act of theirs with a measured response. And if we hold firm to our ideals and purpose, their resistance will eventually crumble."

"Maybe," said the Dove doubtfully. "But it would save a lot of bloodshed if we agreed to negotiate with the opposition in South Vietnam. After all, they control a good half of the country, and if we offered to let them take part in an interim government, pending elections . . ."

"Why," cried the Hawk angrily, "that would be like letting a fox in the chicken coop! Anyway, they aren't a real government. We all know who's pulling the strings. Remember the lesson of Munich."

"Oh, come now," protested the Dove, "it isn't like Munich at all."

"It certainly is," said the Hawk. "The appeasers sold out to the Nazis at Munich and only whetted their appetite. Are you blind to the lessons of history? Don't you realize the forces of aggression must be contained at the outset?"

"Well," conceded the Dove, "there's some merit in that."

"It's the key to the whole thing," said the Hawk. "Think of the nations that are now straddling the fence. If we don't honor our commitments in Vietnam, what will happen in Thailand. Then Laos. Do you want the forces of aggression to overrun all of Southeast Asia?"

"No, of course not. But . . ."

"Do you want us to withdraw completely from Vietnam and leave those loyal Vietnamese who have counted on our support to the tender mercy of their enemies?"

The Dove sighed. "I guess there's no easy way out. But there are so many unanswered questions."

"The easiest way out," said the Hawk with a paternal smile, "is to stop asking questions. Of course, you have a perfect right to ask them. Even though questioning our Vietnam policy gives aid and comfort to the enemy. And makes him think we are divided, thus encouraging him to continue the war."

"You're right!" said the Dove, lifting his shoulders as though relieved of a burden. "The quickest path to peace is to fight harder. Why, I feel better already."

The Hawk put down his chopsticks, took a sip of tea and beamed proudly at the Dove.

"Let us never forget," he said, "that if we citizens of the People's Republic of China march forward together in unquestioning solidarity, the American aggressors can never win in Vietnam."